READING LEARNING CENTERS FOR THE PRIMARY GRADES

Shirleen S. Wait

THE CENTER FOR APPLIED
RESEARCH IN EDUCATION
West Nyack, New York 10995

10 9 8 7

Library of Congress Cataloging-in-Publication Data

Wait, Shirleen S., 1935–
    Reading learning centers for the primary grades / Shirleen Wait.
        p.   cm.

    1. Classroom learning centers—United States.   2. Reading
(Primary)—United States.   I. Title.
LB3044.72.W35   1992
372.4′1—dc20   91-21213
                                                                          CIP

ISBN 0-87628-794-1

**THE CENTER FOR APPLIED RESEARCH
IN EDUCATION**
West Nyack, NY 10994

On the World Wide Web at http://www.phdirect.com

Printed in the United States of America

To my parents Ruth and Hooks Sasser, who insisted that I go into teaching. Thanks, Mother and Daddy!

ABOUT THE AUTHOR

Shirleen Wait received a doctorate in Reading Education from Florida State University. She has taught in elementary schools as a classroom teacher and a reading specialist. In 1984, her colleagues at Chaires Elementary School in Tallahassee Florida, voted her "Teacher of the Year." She studied the developmental education concept in England and has used learning centers for reading instruction since 1967.

From 1987 to 1990, Dr. Wait was the reading specialist for Project CHILD, a three-year research project that integrates computers into elementary classrooms using a learning center approach. She developed the entire K–5 reading curriculum, which includes hundreds of learning center activities.

ABOUT THE ILLUSTRATOR

Jan Schumacher studied at The University of Iowa and now does illustrations for educators. Her work appears in *The Florida Vocational Journal* and other educational publications. She has also published seasonal greeting cards. Ms. Schumacher lives and works in Tallahassee, Florida.

ABOUT THE CONTENT ARTIST

Cindy Koch received an Elementary Education degree from Florida State University and teaches second grade at Ruediger Elementary School in Tallahassee, Florida. She is a resource teacher for cooperative learning and has served as reading instructor for a Florida State summer program designed to teach the writing, editing, and publishing process to primary children.

Ms. Koch designed the bulletin boards and most of the thematic games for this book.

ABOUT THIS BOOK

If you are a primary teacher, a reading specialist, or a beginning teacher who wants to add pizzazz to your reading program, this book is for you. *Reading Learning Centers for the Primary Grades* will help you design learning centers that will engage your students with valuable activities outside their instructional reading groups. The learning centers described in this book will suit the varied learning styles and ability levels of students in grades 1 to 3.

Your students will look forward to their seatwork as they do these exciting activities while waiting for their reading groups. At reading learning centers, students may choose and read books, play reading games, write creative stories, listen to good literature, create art objects, and take part in dramatics and role-play. Furthermore, the independent learning and decision making required of children at the centers will strengthen their self-concepts.

Perhaps you are already using learning centers successfully in your classroom. If so, you'll be able to use ideas in this book to enrich the centers you've already created. You might even surprise your class by creating a completely new center, such as the Theme Center.

Reading Learning Centers for the Primary Grades is divided into five sections:

- Section 1, "Managing Learning Centers," tells how to organize your classroom to accommodate the centers, set up a schedule for easy manageability, provide materials, keep track of work, and evaluate work done at the centers.

- Section 2, "Organizing Learning Centers," describes inexpensive materials for center activities, and shows how to make inexpensive center storage containers.

- Section 3, "The Learning Centers," describes eight types of learning centers (Teacher, Paper and Pencil, Library, Listening, Computer, Art, Writing, and Theme) and tells how they serve students of varied abilities and learning styles.

- Section 4, "Learning Center Theme Units," describes theme centers for each month. Each theme center is a make-believe setting where children participate in game-like activities and role-play. The themes are:

    School Days (*September*)

    Pumpkin Patch (*October*)

    Indian Tepee (*November*)

    Winter Wonderland (*December and January*)

    St. Valentine's Day and Dental Health Month (*February*)

    Space Ship (*March*)

Spring Time (*April*)

Restaurant (*May*)

Many of the themes relate to science or social studies so that you can incorporate these content areas into your reading curriculum. For instance, plan a science unit on the solar system at the same time you use the Space Ship theme, and students can write, read, and listen to books about space at the centers. For each theme, you are given pictures of two bulletin boards, whole-group activities, ideas for integrating science and social studies, a list of activities for each center, directions for setting up the theme center, and reproducible patterns for making a calendar and theme-related reading games (a matching game, sorting game, board game, and two card games for each theme).

- Section 5, "Learning Center Skill Games," contains directions for making board games, card games, sorting games, and matching games that can be used at any center and during any thematic unit. The games are based on phonics, word recognition, vocabulary, and comprehension skills. Reproducible card patterns, an answer key, and a list of suitable games are provided for each skill.

Reading Learning Centers for the Primary Grades will help you make your students look forward to reading and doing these exciting activities. The reading learning centers will certainly enliven your classroom!

Shirleen Wait

HOW TO USE THIS BOOK

THE BENEFITS OF LEARNING CENTERS

Every child has a favorite way to learn. Some learn best by looking or listening, others by moving, touching, and creating. Teachers who are not aware of learning styles often provide activities for children who learn when they look and listen, but not for those who must move and touch in order to learn. Learning centers can provide important work for children during their reading period. Well-designed centers focus on thinking, reading, writing, listening, touching, creating, and talking to teach a strategy or concept. The centers provide stimulating activities for visual, auditory, kinesthetic, and tactile learners.

This is how learning centers are used in the reading program. After you have provided instruction in reading skills and strategies, the children need to practice those strategies before they are tested. The learning centers provide interesting hands-on activities for children to practice using concepts that you have taught in the instructional groups. They also provide opportunities for children to make choices and decisions as they learn.

EXPLAINING LEARNING CENTERS TO PARENTS

Since learning center activities are different from the worksheets parents are used to seeing, you generally need to explain to parents how the learning centers provide valuable learning experiences for the children. You might send a letter to parents explaining why you are using learning centers. (See the sample letter.) Then, invite parents to an "open house." At the open house, talk about the purpose of each learning center. Have parents and their children work as partners doing simple learning center activities together.

When talking to parents about the learning centers, make the following points:

- All children *can* learn the way they learn best.
- Every child has a favorite way to learn. Learning centers include many kinds of learning activities. At the centers, children look, listen, move, touch, and create as they learn.
- Learning centers foster cooperative learning. Children learn to work together effectively as partners or in small groups to practice what they are taught in their reading group.
- Behavior problems are reduced. Children are allowed to move around, and the motivation and decision making required at the learning centers strengthen their self-concepts.

- Center activities are work. Children do not have to finish their work to select an interesting activity. The learning center activities *are* their work.

HOW TO START USING THE READING LEARNING CENTERS

Even if you have never used learning centers, you can begin immediately with the Teacher Center, Paper and Pencil Center, Library Center, and Listening Center. These centers are easy to set up with simple materials found in most classrooms. It is a good idea to get these centers working well before you create a new center. You can add other centers—Theme Center, Computer Center, Art Center, or Writing Center—until you are providing a balance of activities and all the children are learning through hands-on as well as paper-and-pencil activities.

A LETTER TO PARENTS
ABOUT READING LEARNING CENTERS

Dear Parents,

    I hope that by now your child has told you about the learning centers in our room. Reading is very important and one of my goals is to encourage good reading habits. I try to make our classroom an exciting place where your child will participate in many kinds of learning activities.

    In our classroom, the children sometimes work in a reading group. They also work at learning centers where I provide stimulating learning activities designed to develop reading skills. These activities include not only reading but listening, talking, creating, and writing. Children read books, do hands-on projects, listen to story tapes, and play reading games. They work at the learning centers with a partner or with other students. I encourage them to discuss their work and help each other.

    Learning centers incorporate active learning using hands-on learning projects. So, do not expect to see worksheets coming home every day. I encourage you to come to our "open house" to see the learning centers and participate in a learning center activity with your child. Or call the school to make an appointment to visit and see how the learning centers work. I'll be happy to talk about your child's progress.

Sincerely yours,

_____
Teacher

. . . .

OPEN HOUSE

WHERE _____

WHEN _____

I/WE CAN COME TO THE OPEN HOUSE.   YES   NO   (Circle One.)

NAME(S) _____

_____

ACKNOWLEDGMENTS

Many friends made this book possible. For two years, my husband Pete constructed theme centers in our living room. My parents, Ruth and Hooks Sasser, spent hours making skill game cards. Anne Kanady, Joe Arnett, and JoAnne Arnett offered encouragement and prayers. Drs. Patricia Tolbert, Sara Butzin, and Linda Fisher read manuscripts and added ideas. Diane Holman and Ardyth Ann Stanley shared creative classroom activities. Jan Schumacher and Cindy Koch created beautiful illustrations and activities. Margaret Barlow assisted with editing and Dessa Way prepared the manuscript for typesetting. To each I give thanks.

CONTENTS

4. LEARNING CENTER THEME UNITS • 51

Contents

5. LEARNING CENTER SKILL GAMES • 149

Part II: Game Cards and Answer Keys 162

Abbreviations (163) • Antonyms (168) • Compound
Words (174) • Consonant Blends (180) • Consonant
Digraphs (202) • Contractions (208) • Figurative Language (214)
• Homophones (220) • Syllables (226) • Synonyms (229)

Reproducible Pages
Game Cards   235
Blank Game Cards   236

1. MANAGING LEARNING CENTERS

CREATING AREAS

A learning center is a designated place where children find activities, materials, and directions. Learning centers can work in any classroom because they require no special furniture or arrangement. Some teachers prefer an informal atmosphere in which there are no assigned seats and students keep personal items and school supplies in a box or tote tray. The learning centers are situated in carrels or at tables. Students work in chairs or on the floor at the centers. When children finish at one center they move to another.

Learning centers also work effectively in classrooms where each student has an assigned desk. A center might be a table rather than a carrel; but activities as well as directions and materials are provided. Students work on activities at the center or at their own desks.

You can create center areas without using expensive dividers or furniture. For example, a book cart or bookshelf makes a great Library Center. Put a carpet remnant and cushions on the floor near the books. Children can read on the floor area or at their desks. Place the learning centers wherever you want them—on bookshelves or tables, in baskets, on the floor, or under tables. Get your creative juices flowing. The children will love it!

ACQUIRING LOW-COST FURNITURE

You can make your center areas attractive by using low-cost or free furniture. My favorite Library Center had furniture rescued from a church trash pile. All it required was a home-repair job and a good scrubbing. Parents made cushions from left-over fabric and added a bright carpet remnant. The children were thrilled. Here are some sources for low-cost furniture:

- Parents, colleagues, friends
- Attics, garage sales, flea markets, rummage sales
- Electric and telephone companies and electrical suppliers

(Empty wire spools make great low tables)

ARRANGING THE ROOM

When arranging the classroom for learning centers, you must plan so that the centers are placed correctly for electrical outlets and lighting and that the centers are balanced for noisy versus quiet. These are some practical ideas for you to consider:

- Organize the room into an active half and a quiet half. For instance, put the Listening, Reading, and Writing centers in the quiet half and the Teacher, Art, and Theme centers in the active half.
- Place the Teacher Center where you can see the entire room. When you are working with small groups you can also monitor students as they work at the centers.
- The Reading and Writing Centers need adequate lighting.
- Place the Art Center near the sink.
- Place the Listening and Computer Centers near electrical outlets.
- Locate at least one center on the floor. Children like working at floor centers and this saves furniture for other purposes.
- Organize student desks in clusters rather than in rows. This creates more floor space that can be used for learning centers.

The illustrations on page 3 show two possible floor plans.

PLANNING

Learning centers require structure. You must have an overall plan, know how to execute the plan, and teach the children how to follow the plan. This section describes a 3-stage plan for implementing learning centers.

Before you set up the centers, there are five decisions that you must make, called the "Famous Five." Here they are:

1. Decide which centers you wish to use. Start with four centers. When these four centers are working well, add more centers until you have the number of centers that you want.

2. Decide what behaviors you expect from children while they work at centers. May they talk quietly about their work? Will they work as partners? What will happen if a child does not behave the way you wish?

3. Plan traffic patterns so that children can move easily from one center to another.

4. Decide what a child is to do if he or she has a question about work at the center. Is the child to ask a partner or another child at the center? Is the child to interrupt the teacher?

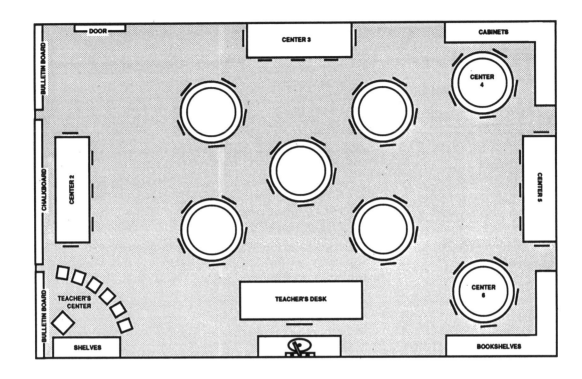

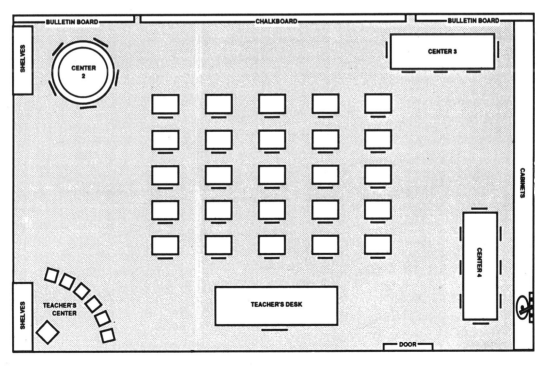

5. Decide what children are to do if they finish their work at a center before it is time to move to another center. Will you provide books or games for them to work with when they finish their center assignment? Also, decide who is going to clean up and where the supplies will be placed.

After you decide how you will execute the "Famous Five," you are ready to begin your plan. If this is your first experience with learning centers, implement your plan in three stages. As you learn to manage one stage, move on to the next.

STAGE 1

Center Visitation

For learning centers to meet the learning styles of all children, you must schedule *every child* to visit each center. (Slower-learning children will learn best when actively involved in center work.) Stage 1 introduces four learning centers. During Stage 1, assign each reading team to a learning center for 20 minutes. At the end of 20 minutes, each team moves to a new center so that in 1 hour and 20 minutes, every team will have visited all four centers. There is nothing sacred about 20 minutes. Shorten or lengthen the time if you wish. It may be best to start with 10 minutes and work up to 20.

Sample Schedule

8:40–9:00	Opening exercises and class meeting
9:00–9:20	First center assignment
9:20–9:40	Second center assignment
9:40–10:00	Recess and snack
10:00–10:20	Third center assignment
10:20–10:40	Fourth center assignment

Implementing Stage 1

1. Divide your class into four reading groups. If you have three groups, make four by dividing your largest group into two groups. Call the groups reading teams. It is important that there are no "Red Birds," "Blue Birds," and "Buzzards."
2. Set up four learning centers—the Teacher center and three other centers.
3. Make an assignment board so that you can easily assign teams without an announcement. (See the illustration.) On a poster board or blackboard, tape 4 envelope pockets, one pocket for each center. Write the name of each reading team on an index card. The index cards fit into the pockets indicating the assignments. Use the assignment board to assign the first centers. Then have a pre-assigned rotation routine, e.g. clockwise.

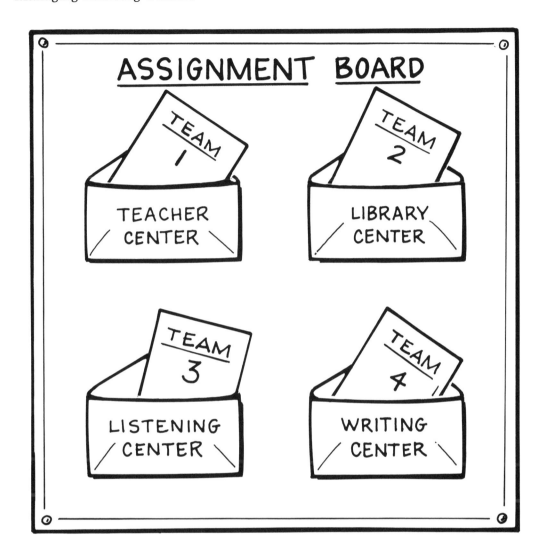

Ten-Day Training Program

Adapted from Project CHILD (Computers Helping Instruction and Learning Development) Courtesy of Sarah Butzin and The Florida Department of Education

Students are expected to work independently or with partners at the centers while you are instructing other small groups. During the ten-day training period, you must train the children in important procedures so that the work at the centers will run smoothly. Ten days may seem like a long time to spend on training, but later you will see that the time was well spent.

Instead of teaching a reading team yourself, spend the first week circulating and helping at the centers. This way, you can observe groups working and stop unwanted behavior.

Day 1   Conduct a class meeting. Announce the team assignments and explain your behavior expectations and traffic patterns to the children. Have each team practice walking from one center to another. Praise good behavior. Then have the children help you develop a set of class rules for working at centers. Write them on a chart and post them.

Day 2   Explain the assignment board. Then, introduce each center to your class. Explain the purpose of each center and show examples of the kind of work that will be done. Explain where to get materials, find the task assignment, and put finished and unfinished work. Have children role play getting materials, putting finished and unfinished work away, and walking to and from the centers.

Role play using a "whisper voice." Many children can read to each other and play games in a whisper voice without disturbing you at the Teacher Center. In fact, they think it is fun. Have a hand signal or bell to use in case the noise level gets too high. Children will immediately know to whisper again.

Days 3–5   Each day, review the rules and expectations. Use the assignment board to assign the children to the four centers. At each center including the Teacher Center, provide an independent activity that can be completed in 20 minutes. If 20 minutes seems too long, change your schedule to 10 or 15 minutes. Circulate, observe, answer questions, and praise good behavior. When center time is over, have a class meeting. Discuss what went well and what needs improvement. Be consistent in enforcing your expectations. It's easier to learn good habits from the beginning than to unlearn bad habits.

Days 6–7   Continue to review the class rules and use the assignment board. If the centers are not functioning well, continue to circulate as you did on Days 3–5. If they are running smoothly, sit with the children at the Teacher Center while they complete their independent activity. Do not teach a reading lesson. Instead, observe the behavior at the other centers to see if teams can work without your immediate supervision.

Days 8–10   Continue to use the assignment board daily. By Day 8 or 9, children should be on task at the learning centers. If they are, begin reading instruction at the Teacher Center. If not, delay reading instruction until children at the centers stay on task. Use Stage 1 until you are comfortable with it and ready to add more centers. This could be several days, weeks, or months.

STAGE 2

Center Visitation

Stage 2 expands the first four centers to include five or six centers. During Stage 2, assign each reading team to a learning center for 20 minutes. Children spend 1 hour and 20 minutes visiting four centers. However, the children do not visit every center every day.

Sample Schedule

Day 1 Children visit centers 1, 2, 3, and 4 (Close 5 and 6.)
Day 2 Children visit centers 1, 2, 5, and 6 (Close 3 and 4.)
Day 3 Children visit centers 3, 4, 5, and 6 (Close 1 and 2.)

When you close the Teacher Center, work with reading teams at other centers such as the Writing Center or the Paper and Pencil Center. You may wish to meet with your low-ability team in the Teacher Center every day. If you do, assign that team to three other centers that are open that day.

Implementing Stage 2

1. Create 1 or 2 new learning centers in addition to your four existing centers.

2. For each new center, tape an additional envelope pocket to the assignment board.

3. Periodically, provide "Free-Choice Friday"! During one or two 20-minute sessions, open all the centers and let children decide which centers to visit. Do not require that reading teams stay together at the centers. If the center is full, allow children to take an activity from the center and work at their desks.

STAGE 3

Center Visitation

Stage 3 expands student choice of centers and incorporates a management chart instead of an assignment board. The management chart is used two ways: (1) as a wall chart for children to check off centers they visit, and (2) as a teacher chart to check off work done at the centers. Reading teams meet with the teacher in the Teacher Center. When children are not in a reading team, they may choose which centers to visit. Reading teams are not required to stay together at the centers. This stage allows children to work with other reading levels so that they are not "tracked" for all of their reading period. For this reason, stage 3 should be your goal, even if it takes awhile.

At first, require children to stay at each center for the full 20-minute session. Then let them choose another center. Provide reading games from Section 5 for those who finish center tasks early. Later, try letting children change centers when they finish their activity, rather than waiting the full 20 minutes.

If a center is full, children can work at a desk or on the floor near the center. You may have to limit the number of children who may work at a particular center (listening or art) to the number of chairs at the center (or put a number card on the wall that tells how many may work at the center).

Allow 1 hour and 20 minutes for students to visit centers. Tell children that they are responsible for visiting every center. Teach them how to keep track of center visits on the management chart. If more than four centers are open, allow 2 days for completing work at the centers.

You may find a few children who need more structure. They cannot handle free choice of centers on a daily basis. Continue to assign them to centers as you did in Stages 1 and 2, but allow them to help you plan their schedule. Give them "Free Choice Friday." If they respond well, add other "Free Choice" days, one at a time, until they are responsible for their own schedule all or most of the time.

Implementing Stage 3

Management chart courtesy of Ardyth Ann Stanley

1. Photocopy the management chart, fill in the students' names, and write the names of the centers in the spaces across the top. Post the chart at eye level. You may want to make a larger version of this chart on poster board.

2. On the blackboard, write the time that each reading team is to meet at the Teacher Center.

3. Have children check the chart to indicate which centers they visited.

Learning Center
Management Chart

Learning Center

Student

PROVIDING MATERIALS

The success of a learning center environment largely depends on the teacher providing material and sufficient directions to keep children motivated and on task. At the Teacher and Paper and Pencil Centers, provide separate assignments for each reading team, at their ability level. Assign work that each team can finish in the 20-minute session. At other centers, provide a variety of activities and have different expectations for different ability levels. For instance, at the Writing Center have every child writing, even though some children are better writers than others.

Every class has fast workers and slow workers. At each center, provide activities from this book for children who have finished their assignment. Allow slow workers to finish at home, during a makeup time, or during the next center visit.

Help children be self sufficient at the centers. Where possible, make the activities self checking. Provide an assignment card with clear directions, answer keys, and samples of finished products—finished products should be basic so that children create their own work and don't copy the finished product. Provide common materials so children do not have to bring anything to the center with them.

KEEPING TRACK OF WORK

Keeping track of each student's work may seem like an impossible task, but it is not. Hands-on activities at the centers cut down on paperwork. At each center where assignments are products, provide containers—boxes, manila folders, or baskets—for finished and unfinished work.

Photocopy the management chart, fill in the student's names, and write the names of products you are checking in the spaces across the top. Each day, spot check the centers and check off successful completions of each child's work. Or have a place in the grade book for center work. As it is done at the end of the day, put a check or grade to let you know it is completed. Toward the end of the week you can see at a glance who needs to complete work or go to a center not yet visited. This is especially important when students are choosing centers. Some centers, such as the Library Center, can be "any time" centers. Students can go there when they finish their work at all the centers.

Provide each child with a portfolio for keeping finished work, and writing samples. Provide each reading team with a box for storing portfolios. Keep the portfolios in a place that is available to you and the children. Allow time each week to distribute work for children to file in their portfolios.

EVALUATING LEARNING
AT THE CENTERS

It is important to give children feedback. Not every activity produces a paper to grade, but there are many other ways to make children aware of their progress. Select two or three ways.

- Self-checking helps children take responsibility for their own learning. It also strengthens their self concepts. Provide ways for children to check their work at the centers. Provide only one activity per day that you must check.

- Teacher observation is a powerful evaluation tool. Every two weeks, plan an observation day. To do this, have children at the Teacher Center read their story to a partner. Use this time to observe children's responses during games and at the other centers.

- The reproducible games in this book have answer keys. Don't make children learn words *before* they can play a game. Allow them to use answer keys to learn while playing the games. As they learn, they will use the answer keys less and less. Note this in your observations.

- Plan weekly conferences with each reading team. Go over work in the portfolios. Let children share some of their products. Praise their achievement and help them decide which centers need more work.

- Some computer programs provide scores. Have children record them on index cards and keep them in their portfolios.

- Display work, record original work on tapes, publish and display writing in the classroom and library, and provide time for children to share work in the class and with other classes.

2. ORGANIZING LEARNING CENTERS

FINDING MATERIALS

COMMERCIAL MATERIALS

Interesting learning centers require a variety of materials. There are many free or inexpensive commercial learning center materials, but sometimes you have to use your imagination to adapt them. Here are a few tips:

- Begin to look at everything—egg cartons, fabric, cereal boxes, etc.—with this idea: How can I use this in a learning center activity?

- Keep an eye out for close-out tables. Frequently, excellent games have been marked down to a fraction of their original cost. Before you buy, check to see that all the game pieces are intact.

- When selecting games, make sure that players must read or use a reading skill in order to play the game.

- Out-of-date basal readers make great story books. Cut out individual stories, staple them, and let the children decorate covers. Or cut out the illustrations and use them with a flannel board.

TEACHER-MADE MATERIALS

Creating learning center materials is time consuming. It is wise to enlist the help of colleagues, parent volunteers, paraprofessionals, and students for creating original, made-to-order materials. Save yourself time by putting the children to work. They can cut and color the reproducibles in this book after you have duplicated them. If you laminate the finished pieces, they will be durable.

ON-GOING MATERIALS

Since finding good activities is sometimes difficult, it is important to have on hand board games, card games, puzzles, and matching activities that can be used over and over. This book is filled with games and activities that children enjoy repeating. You might wish to add interesting puzzles, flash cards, software, slates, commercial games and a flannel board with story pictures.

STORING CENTER MATERIALS

Since learning-center materials include many manipulatives, storage areas are essential. There are several options for storing current center materials and materials not currently being used.

- The board games in this book are made on file folders. Label each file folder with the name of the game board and store it in a file cabinet, a large cardboard box, or a shopping bag.
- Keep game cards in containers that are easy to store—small boxes, labeled envelopes, or self-sealed plastic bags.
- If your room lacks storage space, keep commercial games and puzzles at the centers to be used as ongoing activities.
- Don't store sorting containers. Use the same containers over and over. The label can be easily changed if you attach it to the container with tape, a clothespin or a large paper clip.
- Whenever possible, use shopping bags, plastic self-sealed bags, and envelopes for storage containers. They are easily folded and stored.
- Store activities for themes together so you can gather everything you need at one time. Ditto paper boxes are great for this.

MAKING STORAGE CONTAINERS

You will want attractive containers for storing the center activities. There are many free or low-cost storage containers—shopping bags, stadium cups, envelopes, plastic bags, floral baskets, stationery boxes, coffee cans, cookie tins, ice-cream and popcorn tubs and fruit crates. Following are a few suggestions on using them:

- Envelopes, stationery boxes, and plastic bags to hold card games and matching games
- Cylinder containers to hold sorting games
- Shopping bags to hold board games
- Envelopes or small boxes to hold games
- Baskets to hold the envelopes or boxes

ENVELOPES AND PLASTIC BAGS

Small brown envelopes are inexpensive, easy to decorate, and good for storing card and matching games. Self-sealing plastic bags serve the same purpose and last longer than envelopes. However, the bags cost more than envelopes and cannot be decorated with crayons or markers.

To make envelope containers you will need:

- Brown envelopes
- Crayons or colored marking pens (markers)
- Masking tape
- Hole punch

Directions:

1. Cover the gummed edge of the envelope flap with masking tape. Reopen the hole with a hole punch. This prevents the envelope from sealing, but allows the brad to slip through.
2. With a colored marking pen, write the name of the game on the front of the envelope.
3. Have children decorate the envelopes using crayons or markers.

For plastic-bag containers you will need:

- Self-sealing bags in assorted sizes
- Gummed labels (mailing labels or name tags) and a marker
- Decorative stickers

Directions:

1. Write the name of the game on the label and attach it to the bag.
2. Decorate each bag with a sticker.

STATIONERY BOXES

Store games in small, sturdy, boxes, such as stationery boxes. If the box is pretty, it needs no decoration. All you need to do is label it.

For each box that you wish to decorate you will need:

- Old greeting cards or contact paper
- Scissors
- Glue
- Label and marker

Directions:

1. Have children cut designs from old greeting cards and glue them to the top of the box or cover the box with contact paper.
2. With a colored marker, write the name of the game on the label. Attach the label to the box.
3. Glue the answer key inside the box lid.

CYLINDER CONTAINERS

Use cylinder containers—coffee cans, stadium cups, oatmeal boxes and theater popcorn tubs—for sorting games. Cylinders are easily decorated with paint, stickers, and colored masking tape.

For each container you will need:

- Can, large cup, oatmeal box, or popcorn tub
- Can of spray paint or small can of enamel and paintbrush
- Colored masking tape in a contrasting color
- Decorations such as stickers (optional)
- Label (index card or reproducible sorting-game decoration)

Directions:

1. Clean each container with a dust cloth.
2. Following the directions on the paint can, apply two coats of enamel to the outside of each container. Paint the inside too, if you wish. Allow plenty of time for the paint to dry.
3. Bind the open rim of the container with colored masking tape. This adds a colorful border and prevents cut fingers (coffee cans) and frayed openings (oatmeal boxes).
4. If you wish, decorate the painted container with stickers.
5. Attach a label to each container with a clothespin, tape, or a large paper clip.

SHOPPING BAGS

Shopping bags are good for storing board games because they are large and save space when you hang them on cup hooks at the learning centers.

You will need:

- One or more paper shopping bags or gift-size shopping bags
- Old magazines or greeting cards
- Scissors
- Glue or rubber cement
- Oaktag strip or index card (for a label)
- Cup hook

Directions:

1. Have children cut pictures from the magazines or greeting cards. The pictures can represent a theme such as "Winter Wonderland."
2. Have them create a winter scene by gluing the pictures onto the shopping bag.
3. Describe the contents of the storage bag on the label, e.g., "Board Games."
4. Glue the label to the front of the bag.
5. Hang the bag on a cup hook at the learning center.

Baskets

Baskets are great for storing games that are in small boxes or plastic bags. They usually need little or no decoration.

For each basket you will need:

- Index card (label) and marker
- Hole punch
- Ribbon

Directions:

1. Write the contents of the basket on the index card.
2. Punch a hole in the card and tie it to the basket handle with a colorful ribbon.

3. THE LEARNING CENTERS

This section gives the purpose of each learning center and complete instructions and diagrams for setting up the centers.

TEACHER CENTER

The Teacher Center is one of the easiest to create. Most classrooms already have a reading circle or table. By adding a few materials you can make your circle into an attractive and exciting center where you can meet with reading and literature groups. Here, children learn the reading skills that they will be practicing independently or with partners at the other centers.

Most reading groups meet to read and to do follow-up pencil and paper activities—both visual activities. To be exciting, the Teacher Center also should contain a rich variety of additional visual, auditory, kinesthetic, and tactile materials for the teacher to use with each group of readers.

Visual and Auditory Materials

It is easy to expand visual activities and make them auditory:

Children love to sing songs. Make singing an auditory reading activity by printing songs on charts and pointing to the words as the group sings. This activity also works well with rhymes, jump-rope chants, school cheers, and poems. You'll be surprised at how quickly children learn vocabulary this way. If you can't sing, play a record or tape and sing along, pointing to the words.

"Big books" are large-size books created for choral reading and reading to groups of students. They are designed to be used in visual-auditory activities. The big book rests on a stand or easel and the teacher or a child points to the words as the group reads. Children quickly learn to chime in and read aloud with the teacher. They love to take turns pointing to the words (kinesthetic and tactile). Before you know it, the whole class is reading together in this visual-auditory activity.

Although you can buy big books from publishers and retail stores, it is easy and fun to make your own. Use chart paper and colored markers for printing stories, rhymes, and songs (or anything you wish) into the big books. Let the children illustrate the pages and fasten them together with rings or yarn.

Kinesthetic and Tactile Materials

Many children learn best through moving and touching, so it is important to include kinesthetic and tactile materials at the Teacher Center:

- To make your singing activities kinesthetic and tactile as well as visual or auditory, use simple rhythm instruments. Team an Indian chant with instruments made from oatmeal boxes and pencils. Or have children create "instant instruments" by tapping pencils or fingers, shaking keys or change purses, or clapping their hands. The point is to get some body action into the reading lesson.

- Children learn quickly through games, so take time to play hands-on games at the Teacher Center. Use games from the Theme Center, commercial games, or games you create especially for each group. Well-designed games teach decision-making and critical-thinking as well as reading skills.

- Pocket charts are available at most schools. You can make your pocket chart into a kinesthetic and tactile reading activity in which children move sentence strips and vocabulary cards. Have children complete sentences, fill in blanks, match compound words, etc.

- A flannel board works as well as a pocket chart and is easy to make. Children can sequence pictures, match sentences to story pictures, and tell stories on the flannel board.

Directions for Making a Flannel Board

Materials:

- 1 piece ⅜ inch plywood, 2 ft. by 4 ft.
- solid-color flannel, 4 in. longer and wider than plywood
- staple gun and staples

Directions:

1. Lay material flat on the floor. Lay the plywood flat on the material so that 2 inches of the material shows all around the plywood.
2. Fold excess flannel over edge of the plywood. Pull the flannel taut, turn under the raw edges, miter the corners, and staple it to the plywood.

Pictures that adhere to a flannel board:

- felt shapes
- pictures from old magazines, basal readers, or greeting cards backed with flannel
- interfacing fabric decorated with markers and glitter

TEACHER CENTER SET-UP

You'll need:

- Student seating, either a table and chairs or semicircle of chairs
- Teacher chair
- Chart stand
- Easel or stand for big books, flannel board, and pocket chart (a chalk rail works well)
- Storage shelf

Materials for the teacher center:

- Instructional materials
- Pocket chart, sentence strips, and vocabulary cards—make special cards from each theme by copying key words from game cards onto index cards.
- Flannel board and story pictures
- Rhythm instruments
- Games

- Basket to store envelopes and boxes of games
- Boxes to store story pictures, instruments, sentence strips, and vocabulary cards
- Labels
- A poster or sign that says "Teacher Center"

Directions:

1. Arrange student seating in an area with good lighting.
2. Position your chair so that all the centers are in view. Place the chart stand and easel next to your chair.
3. Put the storage shelf nearby to hold books and boxes of story pictures, instruments, etc.
4. Stand the big books, flannel board, and extra charts next to a nearby wall.
5. Describe the contents of each box on a label ("Rhythm Instruments," "Story Pictures," "Pocket Chart Cards"). Glue a label to each box and store the boxes on the shelf.
6. Post the signs.

THEME-RELATED ACTIVITIES FOR THE TEACHER CENTER

For every theme:

- Play pocket-chart games using vocabulary from the theme—(Write sentences or key words from game cards on sentence strips.)
- Demonstrate hands-on games made from reproducibles for the theme.
- Tell flannel-board stories related to the theme.
- Make story charts with theme-related stories created by the reading groups.
- Create and read theme-related big books.
- Sing songs using song charts.

September—School Days

Create an alma mater and a school cheer for the song chart.

October—Pumpkin Patch

Use musical instruments (such as maracas) made from gourds.

November—Indian Tepee

Create Indian chants for the song chart—spray-paint coffee cans to use as Indian drums.

December and January—Winter Wonderland

Use Christmas bells for musical instruments and demonstrate winter equipment such as ice skates or skis.

February—St. Valentine's Day and Dental Health Month

Create a dental health "rap" and a Valentine song for the song chart.

March—Space Ship

Create a space-ship choral reading for the song chart.
Learn to read the names of galaxies, planets, and star formations.

April—Spring Time

Act out a spring play from a basal reader.
Write a group story about planting seeds.

May—Restaurant

Sing restaurant commercials using song charts—use kitchen items such as spoons for musical instruments.

PAPER AND PENCIL CENTER

Your children probably work at their desks doing paper-and-pencil activities when they are not in their reading groups. In a learning-center classroom, where the teacher provides a variety of types of opportunities for learning, paper and pencil activities are balanced with active learning at the other centers. So make brief, meaningful assignments and select only the most interesting, useful worksheets and workbook pages for this center.

PAPER AND PENCIL CENTER SET-UP

You will need:

- Student seating, either a table and chairs or a group of desks
- Chalkboard
- Shelf

Materials for the paper and pencil center:

- Jar of pencils with erasers, crayons, paper
- Boxes or manila folders for finished and unfinished work
- Labels
- Plants for decoration
- Poster or sign that says "Paper and Pencil Center"
- Student assignments (on the chalkboard)

Directions:

1. Arrange student seating and the shelf near the chalkboard.
2. Label the boxes or manila folders.
3. Store the pencils, crayons, paper, and containers for work on the shelf. Decorate the shelf with plants.
4. Post the sign and write student assignments on the chalkboard.

THEME-RELATED ACTIVITIES FOR THE PAPER AND PENCIL CENTER

For every theme:

- Assign basal reader paper and pencil activities as well as worksheet and board-work activities that relate to the theme.
- Fill in the calendars from this book.

LIBRARY CENTER

The more children read, the more their reading skills improve. You'll be delighted at the number of children who will read when they can choose their own books and read them as part of their daily work. Provide easy books so children can read independently. Include cartoon and joke books. Children will read these over and over.

Encourage children to keep a record of the books they have read at the center. Make a booklet for each student by stapling together several sheets of lined paper, making a construction paper cover, and writing *Books I Have Read* on the cover. Students can write the title, author, and the date they finish in this booklet.

No doubt, children who visit the Library Center will want to borrow books. Keep a sheet of paper and a pencil handy so the children can write their name and the name of the book they are borrowing.

LIBRARY CENTER SET-UP

You will need:

- Student seating, either a table and chairs, an area rug, cushions, bean-bag chairs, or carpeting squares
- Bookshelves or book cart
- Wall space for charts and big books introduced in the Teacher Center

Materials for the Library Center:

- Primary reading materials—big books, charts, books, catalogs, telephone books, cookbooks, menus, children's magazines and newspapers, maps, globes, children's reference books, cartoon books, and books written by the students
- Books that correlate with the Theme Center
- Shelf labels ("Cookbooks," "Animal Stories," etc.)
- Poster or sign that says "Library Center"
- Poster or sign that says "Don't be a Library Litterbug. Put your books away."
- Sign-up sheet and pencil for those who wish to borrow books

Directions:

1. Arrange student seating near the bookshelves.
2. Organize the reading materials on the bookshelves. Attach labels to the shelves.
3. Post the objective and signs.
4. Put the sign-up sheet and pencil on top of the bookcase.

THEME-RELATED ACTIVITIES FOR THE LIBRARY CENTER

For every theme:

- Provide books from the library.
- Join a children's trade-book club. Some book clubs offer a free classroom book for every ten student books ordered.
- Search flea markets and garage sales where children's books are plentiful and inexpensive.
- Cut out separate stories from outdated basal readers. Staple each story together. Create a cover using wallpaper.

- Move charts and big books from the Teacher Center to the Library Center.
- Create small versions of songs, rhymes, chants, and big books used at the Teacher Center. Because children like to read these over and over, they provide excellent practice.
- Display books that students create in the Writing Center.
- Collect catalogs, telephone books, cookbooks, children's magazines and newspapers, menus, etc.
- Collect maps, globes, and reference books.
- Make cartoon books by cutting cartoons from magazines and newspapers and pasting them into notebooks.

September—School Days

Read newspapers or magazines that feature back-to-school clothing and school supplies.

October—Pumpkin Patch

Read fall seed catalogs and pumpkin cookbooks created by classmates.

November—Indian Tepee

Display children's totem poles for everyone to read.

December and January—Winter Wonderland

Read holiday books and toy catalogs.

February—St. Valentine's Day and Dental Health Month

Read Valentine messages and dental-health brochures.

March—Space Ship

Read children's encyclopedias with articles on space, planets, stars and science books with chapters on space.

April—Spring Time

Read spring seed catalogs.

May—Restaurant

Read food and nutrition books, menus, and magazines that feature food.

LISTENING CENTER

In a Listening Center, children experience regular auditory activities, which can increase their ability to listen effectively. Listening also builds their background knowledge, increases their vocabulary, and is a good way to expose children to good literature.

This center is easy to create because tape recorders and headphones are available in most schools. With a multiple headphone jack, several children can listen to a story using one tape recorder. Place this center near an electrical outlet. The children can sit at a table or on floor cushions or an area rug.

LISTENING CENTER SET-UP

You will need:

- Student seating, either a table and chairs, an area rug, beanbag chairs, stools, cushions, or carpet squares
- Electrical outlet
- One or more tape players

- Multiple-headphone jack and headphones for each tape player
- Filmstrip viewer and filmstrips with tapes (optional)

Materials for the Listening Center:

- Red and green round stickers, one each, to mark tape-recorder buttons
- Books with matching audiotapes—both commercial sets and those created by the teacher and students
- Plastic self-sealing bags and labels
- Clothesline, clothespins, and two large screw eyes
- Poster or sign that says "Listening Center"
- Poster or sign that says "Rewind your tape and put it away."
- If there is an assignment, write it on a large index card.

Directions:

1. Arrange student seating near an electrical outlet.
2. To help children remember which buttons to push, stick a green circle on "forward" and a red circle on the "reverse" button of the tape player. Plug the headphone jack and headphones into the tape player and set it on the table or floor where the children will sit. When headphones are not in use, hang them over the chair backs or the table's edge.
3. Make a clothesline. Install the screw eyes, several feet apart, into a wooden molding or window sill near the center. Thread the clothesline through both screw eyes and tie a knot around each screw eye.
4. Label each bag with the name of a story. Place each matching set—book and tape or filmstrip and tape—in a separate plastic bag. Seal the bags and hang them on the clothesline with clothespins.
5. Post the objective, signs, and student assignment.

THEME-RELATED ACTIVITIES FOR THE LISTENING CENTER

For every theme:

- Provide an assortment of tapes, read-alongs, and filmstrips.
- Have children record books that they have written. Or record a book together by reading along with the student. Then discuss the story and praise the student (on tape). Use the clothesline to store each book and tape for all students to enjoy.

- Make tapes of big books and charts created at the Teacher Center.
- Create small versions of big books and matching tapes.
- Check out books with matching audiotapes from your media center.
- Create audiotapes based on favorite books and basal-reader stories.
- Record some class singing and choral-reading sessions. Make books to match the recordings.
- Include filmstrips with audiotapes. (optional)

September—School Days

Listen to tapes of the alma mater and school songs.

October—Pumpkin Patch

Record spooky stories.

November—Indian Tepee

Record and listen to Indian chants.
Make tapes to go with totem pole stories.

December and January—Winter Wonderland

Listen to holiday songs.

February—St. Valentine's Day and Dental Health Month

Record Valentine messages and the dental-health rap written at the Teacher Center.

March—Space Ship

Listen to tapes, read-alongs, and filmstrips about outer space.

April—Spring Time

Listen to Easter songs and poems.

May—Restaurant

Record and listen to restaurant commercials.
Have students record their menus on tape.

COMPUTER CENTER

If you really want to turn children on to learning, create a learning center with computers. The computer is a powerful learning tool because it allows for several learning styles to be active at once. Not only do children use thinking, reading, listening, moving, and touching when learning a skill on the computer, most children are highly motivated by the computer graphics and formats. Furthermore, the computer's instant feedback makes the learning interactive.

If you decide to create a Computer Center, you'll need to find good software. For your program, you'll want to build a collection of computer activities in these areas, (1) phonics and word analysis, (2) vocabulary, and (3) comprehension, (4) word processing. Also, software that makes banners, posters, and greeting cards is quite useful.

Software may seem expensive, but it really is a bargain. You can offset the cost of software by buying less ditto paper. You will probably use fewer worksheets because paper-and-pencil activities will be balanced with active learning at the centers. Children use paper only once but a software program lasts for many years.

Here are some ideas to get you started.

- Check your media center.
- Ask the district computer specialist whether free or low-cost software is available.
- Read software and trade-book catalogs.
- Find out if software is available for your basal reader.

If the computer is new to your classroom, teach the children how to use it before you create the Computer Center. If possible, instruct small groups of children outside the reading period. At first, have a resource person help you manage this center. Older students, parent volunteers, or teacher's aides make excellent resource people.

Students can use the computer more often if they work with partners or in small groups. Post a list of partners and set a timer for 9–10 minutes. When one pair finishes, they quietly signal the next pair on the list. Students waiting for computer can read, work with puzzles and games, or work at another center.

If your school has a computer lab, use it as an off-site Computer Center. Arrange to rotate small groups of students on a regular basis for computer reading activities. Work with the person in charge to choose a balance of activities that include the three areas (1) phonics and word analysis, (2) vocabulary, and (3) comprehension.

Many computer activities do not require a printer. You may want to add one later on so that students can write and print their own stories, poems, and reports.

COMPUTER CENTER SET-UP

You will need:

- Student seating, two chairs for each computer
- Electrical outlet
- One or more computers, each with a power strip
- Table to hold the computers
- Printer, earphones (optional)

Materials for the Computer Center:

- Appropriate software and software storage boxes
- Computer paper
- Poster or sign that says "Computer Center"
- Chart listing names of partners
- Poster or sign with student directions, "When you finish, signal the next set of partners."

- Timer(s)
- Student assignment (Use a sentence strip and tape it to the wall behind the computer.)

Directions:

1. Place the table near an electrical outlet. The table must be approximately two inches from the wall to allow the computer paper to feed into the printer.
2. Arrange the computer(s), software storage boxes, timer, earphones, and printer on the table. Provide two chairs for each computer.
3. Put the box of computer paper underneath the printer. Feed paper into the printer following the instructions provided with the printer.
4. Post the objective, signs, assignment, and list of partners.

THEME-RELATED ACTIVITIES FOR THE COMPUTER CENTER

For every theme:

- Provide skills practice using vocabulary, comprehension, phonics, and word analysis software.
- Have children use word-processing software for writing.
- Let children use card-maker software.

September—School Days

Write back-to-school stories.

October—Pumpkin Patch

Write spooky stories and create pumpkin posters.

November-Indian Tepee

Write Thanksgiving stories and create greeting cards.

December and January—Winter Wonderland

Write letters to Santa and create holiday greeting cards.

February—St. Valentine's Day and Dental Health Month

Write Valentine messages and create valentines and dental-health posters.

March—Space Ship

Write outer-space stories and create space-ship posters.

April—Spring Time

Write spring stories and create Easter cards and Earth-Day posters.

May—Restaurant

Write a list of favorite foods and create menus.

ART CENTER

At the Art Center, children respond to reading by creating visual expressions of ideas and feelings about what they have read. Art is especially meaningful for kinesthetic and tactile learners because it requires touching and moving as well as visualizing, thinking, and planning. Art activities should tie in directly to what the students are reading and learning.

ART CENTER SET-UP

You will need:

- Student seating, either a table and chairs or a cluster of desks
- Easel (optional)
- Storage shelves
- Art supplies
- Newspapers for covering the desks and table
- Cans for mixing paint and soaking paintbrushes
- Baby food jars to hold paint at the easel
- Painting smock (adult shirt turned backwards)
- Poster or sign that says "Art Center"
- List of student names—students put a check by their name after they have used the easel
- Poster or sign with student directions, "When you finish, put your materials away."
- Student assignment (Use a sentence strip and post it near the center.)

Directions:

1. If you have a sink in your room, arrange student seating near it. Cover the table top or desk tops with newspaper.
2. Hang the smock on the corner of the easel and place the easel near the student work area. While one child uses the easel, a small group works at the table. Put three or four half-filled paint jars in the easel paint holders. Provide one paint brush for each color of paint.
3. Fill the labeled boxes and jars and store them on the shelves. It is not necessary that the storage shelves be at the Art Center. You may wish to use your storage closet for the art materials and bring out only those materials needed for an activity.
4. Post the objective, signs, assignments, and check-off sheet.

THEME-RELATED ACTIVITIES FOR THE ART CENTER

For every theme:

- Illustrate and make covers for students-written books.
- Make puppets of characters.

- Build story settings in shoe boxes.
- Assemble and decorate a class telephone directories, recipe books, etc.
- Create and illustrate books about the classroom theme.
- Illustrate music and poetry.
- Create book jackets for favorite books. Include the names of the author, illustrator, and publisher.
- Decorate calendars from this book.

September—School Days

Decorate portfolios for storing work.

Create collages using newspaper ads of back-to-school clothing.

Embroider simple samplers or create hornbooks.

Decorate journal covers.

October—Pumpkin Patch

Design covers for pumpkin recipe books.

Make pumpkins and jack-o'-lanterns using playdough, clay, paper, or fabric.

Make individual scarecrows or scarecrow puppets using ice cream sticks, fabric, yarn, glue, etc.

Make paper-bag masks. Cut holes for eyes, nose, and mouth in a paper bag. Decorate front and back of bag with crayons and markers.

November—Indian Tepee

Make Indian head dresses and Pilgrim hats.

Decorate Thanksgiving menus.

Create Indian necklaces from dyed macaroni.

December and January—Winter Wonderland

Draw and color ice skaters and snowmen for the winter scene.

Decorate holiday greeting cards and ornaments.

Make playdough snowmen. (See playdough recipe below.)

Make paper snowflakes.

February—St. Valentine's Day and Dental Health Month

Create room decorations.

Create Valentines.

Make dental-health posters.

March—Space Ship

Create a class mural of the solar system. (Use butcher paper or cloth and colored markers.)

Make playdough models of the stars and planets.

April—Spring Time

Dye eggs or make them from playdough.

May—Restaurant

Decorate menus and place mats.

Decorate recipe books and make book covers.

Create collages using magazine pictures of food.

Make mobiles of favorite foods. Make foods from playdough and hang on a coat hanger with yarn.

Playdough Recipe

Courtesy of Linda Fisher

Mix together until smooth:

1 Cup salt

2 Cups flour

2 Tbsp alum

2 Tbsp salad oil

Cake coloring

1 Cup water—add color to water before mixing

This will stay soft for several weeks.

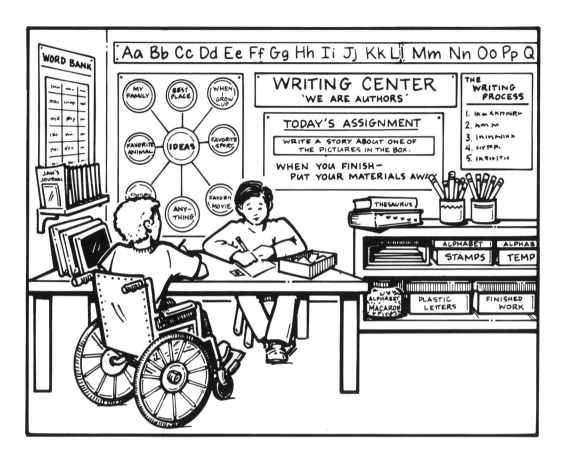

WRITING CENTER

Writing is very important to growth in reading because a *good* writing program increases the amount of time that children spend with text. The Writing Center can play an important role in your reading program because it provides children with opportunities to create their own text and to read what they have written and what their classmates have written.

Writing is a process that develops very much like reading and talking. These language processes develop through maturity, experience, and practice. Some children have many experiences writing at home—notes to Grandma, messages to their parents, grocery lists, etc. They spell some words correctly and invent ways to spell others. Other children who haven't had opportunities to write don't write well at first, but if given a chance these children can become writers, too. So make writing assignments that encourage children to write what they can say. This means accepting invented spelling and less-than-perfect sentence structure. If you require perfect writing the children will not experiment with writing but will write only what they already know how to write. Keep in mind that the more children experiment with writing, the more accomplished they become.

WRITING CENTER SET-UP

You will need:

- Student seating, a table and chairs or a cluster of desks
- Table or storage shelf for supplies

Materials for the Writing Center:

- Writing materials—lined and unlined paper, pencils, markers, crayons
- Manipulatives for letter formation—plastic and macaroni letters, letter stamps, and templates for tracing letters, make-words games and puzzles
- Alphabet, upper- and lowercase
- Posters with list of high-frequency words, descriptive words, and children's names
- Dictionaries and beginning thesauruses
- Boxes or manila folders for finished and unfinished work
- Poster or sign that says "Writing Center"
- Poster or sign with student directions, "When you finish, put your materials away."
- Student assignment (Use a large index card and tape it to the table.)

Directions:

1. Place the student seating near a wall. Post the word lists on the wall.
2. Position the storage table or shelf nearby. Arrange the paper, slates, dictionaries, manipulatives, and jars of writing tools on the storage table.
3. Put the folders for finished and unfinished work in the middle of the writing table.
4. Post the objective, student assignment and signs.

THEME-RELATED ACTIVITIES FOR THE WRITING CENTER

For every theme:

- Write theme books, stories, plays, raps, poems, and songs.
- Write in journals.
- Respond to reading in journals—tell the best part of the story, describe characters and settings, tell the most exciting event, etc.
- Make lists—story facts, things to do, favorite foods, etc.

- Write skits or radio plays to perform for the class.
- Make greeting cards.
- Write letters or messages.
- Make labels for the classroom.
- Write announcements.
- Make posters to display in the classroom.
- Write news stories for the class newspaper.

September—School Days

Make and illustrate a book about favorite school activities.

October—Pumpkin Patch

Keep journal records on the growth of pumpkin vines.
Make a booklet about pumpkins.

November—Indian Tepee

Write a Thanksgiving book.
Write stories using Indian Symbols.

December and January—Winter Wonderland

Create holiday greeting cards.
Write letters to Santa.
Make and illustrate winter activity books.

February—St. Valentine's Day and Dental Health Month

Create Valentine messages for pen pals and classmates.
Create dental-health booklets.

March—Space Ship

Create a space booklet.
Write a message to an astronaut.
List facts about planets.

April—Spring Time

Create an Earth-Day booklet.
Write a spring skit.

May—Restaurant

Create menus.

Create a party invitation that includes their favorite menu.

THEME CENTER

Children learn language through creative play and hands-on games. So why not use games and role-play to create daily reading opportunities? Every month, the Theme Center sets an imaginative new theme for the entire classroom. (See Section 4.) The center also serves as a setting where children engage in active learning through reading games and role play. Props in the center stimulate children's imaginations. Children learn reading skills while pretending they are in a restaurant, post office, or Indian tepee.

In addition to props, the Theme Center also contains hands-on games which provide practice in reading skills that children are learning in their reading groups. There are five specially designed games for each theme. Multiple copies of each game can be reproduced so that several groups of children can play the same game at the same time.

The Theme Center is easy to develop if you do it in stages. The first year, chose three or four themes that are right for your purposes. Use each theme for two or three months. Keep those same themes for the next year and choose three more. Soon you will have enough props to have a new Theme Center each month. Better yet, work with another teacher to create and exchange Theme Centers. Each teacher creates three different theme centers so you have access to six in all.

These are the basic requirements for a Theme Center:

- *Student seating,* either a table and chairs, an area rug, cushions, or carpeting squares
- *Floor space* to set up the theme decorations
- *Labeled containers* to store theme-related games and activities
- *Wall space* to post student directions or a management chart designed to relate to the theme

For each theme you will find:

- a board game pattern
- game cards for making two card games, a sorting game, and a matching game
- sorting-game labels

- matching-game patterns
- a calendar

ASSEMBLING THEME CENTER GAMES

Board Games

1. Copy and decorate the game board master.
2. Glue the two board-game halves inside a file folder and trim protruding edges. Write the name of the game on the front of the folder.
3. Copy the game-board directions and glue them on the back of the folder.
4. Copy the theme game cards on card stock. Laminate the sheets if desired, and cut them apart on the lines to form cards.
5. Glue a small brown envelope to the back of the folder to hold game cards and the answer key. Laminate the game board and slit the film at the envelope's opening.

Rules:

Two or three players may play this game. You will need a game board, game cards, an answer key, one die, and a marker for each player.

1. Each player picks a marker and places it on START.
2. Players roll the die. The player with the highest number will go first. Play clockwise.
3. Each player rolls the die, draws a card, and reads it.
4. If the player reads the card correctly, he or she moves ahead the number shown on the die. If the card is read incorrectly, the player does not move.
5. The player puts the card at the bottom of the pile.
6. The first player to reach FINISH wins!

Card Games

Each theme has two card games.

The object of the card game is to match pairs of cards. For that reason, each page of game cards (15 cards to a page) is copied twice to make 15 *pairs* of cards (one card game).

1. Select one page of game cards. Copy the page on two pieces of card stock to make 15 pairs of cards. Laminate the sheets if desired, and cut them apart on the lines to form cards.

2. Use a small box (such as a stationery box), a small brown envelope, or a self-sealing plastic bag for storing the cards. Decorate the top of the box on the front of the envelope or plastic bag.

3. Copy the card-game directions and glue them inside the box top, on the back of the envelope, or glue on tagboard and place inside the plastic bag.

Rules:

Two players may play. Players will need game cards.

1. Deal five cards to each player. Stack the rest of the cards face down.

2. Player 1 draws one card from the stack. The player then discards one unwanted card face up beside the stack.

3. The other player draws one card—from the stack or from the top of the discard pile—and then discard one unwanted card.

4. When players get a match, they put the pair down on the table.

5. The first player to lay all of his or her cards on the table wins!

Sorting Games

1. Copy and color the sorting game patterns. Attach each pattern to the top edge of a cylinder container with clothespins or jumbo paper clips.

2. Copy both pages of game cards on card stock. Laminate the sheets and cut them apart on the lines to form cards.

3. Use a small brown envelope or self-sealing plastic bag for storing the cards.

4. Glue the game directions on the back of the envelope or glue on tagboard and place inside the plastic bag.

5. Copy the answer key and glue it on tagboard. Place the key inside the envelope or plastic bag.

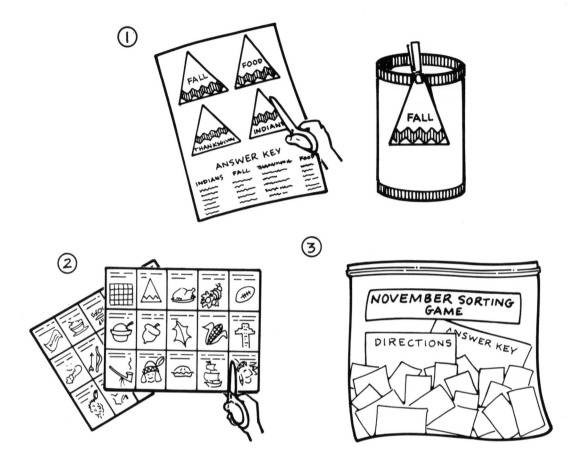

Rules:

One to two players may play this game.

1. Look at the game cards. Decide which category each card matches. Put the card in that container.
2. When you have sorted all the cards, get out the answer key.
3. Read the cards to a partner.

Matching Games

1. Make enough copies of the matching-game patterns so that there is one pattern for every word pair on the answer key. Write a word pair on each pattern.
2. On the back of the pattern, write matching numbers on each side of the matching pair. This allows players to check for correct and incorrect matches by matching numbers. Color and laminate patterns, then cut them apart on the dotted line.
3. Decorate a stationery box, envelope, or self-sealing plastic bag for storing the cards.
4. Copy the game directions and answer key and glue them to the box or envelope or laminate them and put them inside the plastic bag.

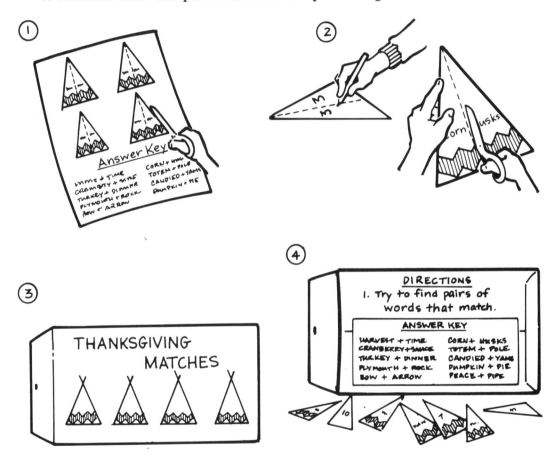

Rules:

Find pairs of words that match.

4. LEARNING CENTER THEME UNITS

SEPTEMBER—SCHOOL DAYS

Theme Decorations   Classroom

Materials for the game area:

- Basic equipment
- School Days board game, card games, sorting game, and matching game
- Learning Center Skills Games (See Section 5.)
- September vocabulary cards (Use game cards or write underlined words from game cards on index cards.)
- A sign that says "We practice reading."

- Poster or sign with student directions, "1. Read a story with the teacher of the day. 2. Read the September vocabulary cards to a partner. 3. Play a reading game."
- Teacher Chart—List children's names under "Teacher of the Day" and write the day of the week that the child will be teacher.

Materials for the school:

- Teacher's desk (table and chair)
- Props—plastic apple, glasses frames, stamp and stamp pad
- Song and story charts with pointer
- Flannel board and story pictures (See flannel board directions, Section 3, Teacher Center.)
- Basal readers (children reread their story with the teacher of the day)
- Slates, chalk, and erasers
- Old workbook or worksheet pages for "playing" school
- Jar of pencils with erasers

Theme Set-Up

1. Position the "teacher's" desk and props near the student seating. Put pointer, pencils, and labeled boxes containing slates, worksheets, and vocabulary cards nearby.
2. Place the song and story charts and flannel board near the student seating.
3. Post objective, student directions, and "Teacher of the Day" chart. The teacher of the day straightens the area before moving to another center.

Bulletin Boards

See the illustrations on page 54.

Whole-Group Activities

- Learn new vocabulary (Chalkboard, workbook, etc).
- Role-play activities that students will use at the theme center (thematic games, big books, vocabulary cards, flannel board).
- Role-play being "teacher of the day" at the theme center.
- Visit the principal's office. Have the principal tell why he or she became a teacher.
- Have the special area teachers (music, art, physical education) tell the class why they became teachers.

- Have a child's grandparent or great grandparent tell the class about his or her school days.
- Create and post a set of class rules.
- Learn the purpose of old-fashioned samplers. (Colonial children embroidered numerals and the ABCs.)
- Create an alma mater by writing words to a familiar tune. Write the words on a song chart.
- Set up overhead projector, screen, transparencies, and pointers. Let students learn current vocabulary and other skills on the screen. Later they can use this activity in pairs.
- Decorate the September calendar.

Content Area Activities

- Study schools in colonial times.
- Learn about schools in other countries.
- Use an encyclopedia to gather information about early books such as the hornbook, *Blueback Speller,* and *McGuffey's Readers.*
- Provide math story problems. (Dan brought the teacher an apple. Bill brought her 4 pears. How many snacks did she have in all?)
- Gather information about the children's favorite school activities. Use the results to create a graph.
- Create a map of the school.
- Create a day's schedule. What time do we read, have recess, go to the lunchroom, go home?

Theme Center Activities

- Reread basal stories with the teacher of the day.
- Take turns role-playing teacher and student.
- Play skill games that reinforce skills being taught in the reading groups.
- Play the School Days board game, card games, sorting game, and matching game.
- Read September vocabulary cards.

September Bulletin Boards

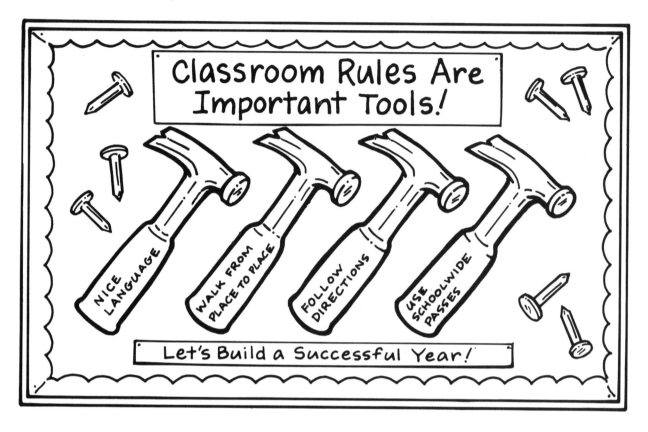

Classroom Rules Are Important Tools!

NICE LANGUAGE

WALK FROM PLACE TO PLACE

FOLLOW DIRECTIONS

USE SCHOOLWIDE PASSES

Let's Build a Successful Year!

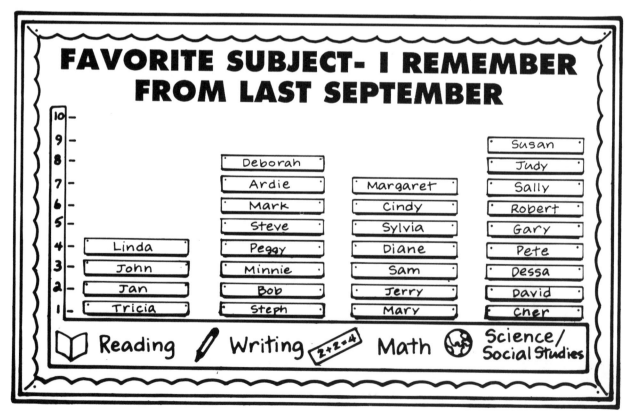

FAVORITE SUBJECT- I REMEMBER FROM LAST SEPTEMBER

	Reading	Writing	Math	Science/Social Studies
10				
9				Susan
8		Deborah		Judy
7		Ardie	Margaret	Sally
6		Mark	Cindy	Robert
5		Steve	Sylvia	Gary
4	Linda	Peggy	Diane	Pete
3	John	Minnie	Sam	Dessa
2	Jan	Bob	Jerry	David
1	Tricia	Steph	Mary	Cher

SEPTEMBER

SUNDAY	MONDAY	TUESDAY	WEDNESDAY	THURSDAY	FRIDAY	SATURDAY

Take A Ride on th

START →

A⁺
on your
test!
Roll again.

FINISH
YOU
WIN!

Forgot
your
lunch!
Lose one
turn.

LUNCH

e September School Bus

Talking too loud. Move back two.

Game Cards

Honor Roll! Move ahead one.

TEXT BOOK

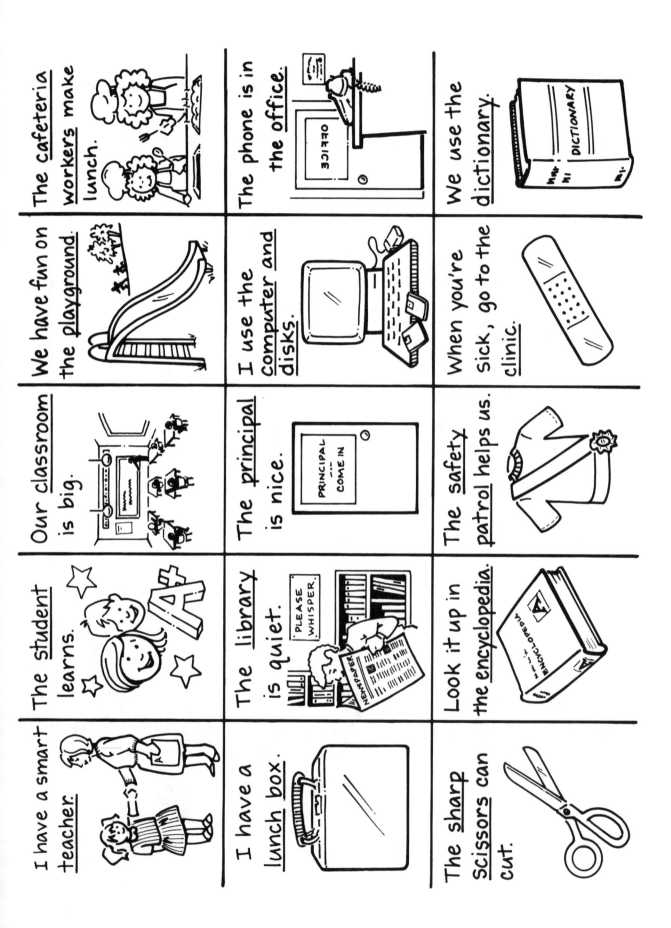

I have a smart teacher.	The student learns.	Our classroom is big.	We have fun on the playground.	The cafeteria workers make lunch.
I have a lunch box.	The library is quiet.	The principal is nice.	I use the computer and disks.	The phone is in the office.
The sharp scissors can cut.	Look it up in the encyclopedia.	The safety patrol helps us.	When you're sick, go to the clinic.	We use the dictionary.

Sit at the desk.

Science is interesting.

Physical education is outside.

I have some color crayons.

He loves writing stories.

Music class is fun.

The eraser is important.

Reading books is fun.

Walk to the art room.

Write on the paper.

Use the card catalog.

Use the sticky glue.

I see a lead pencil.

The chalkboard is big.

Social Studies is important.

September Sorting Game

School Tools

Places

People

Activities

School Tools	Places	Activities	People
lead pencil	art room	reading books	teacher
paper	music class	writing stories	student
eraser	classroom	science	principal
color crayons	playground	social studies	safety patrol
desk	library	physical	cafeteria
chalkboard	office	education	worker
card catalog	clinic		
sticky glue			
lunch box			
sharp scissors			
dictionary			
encyclopedia			
computer			
and disks			

Answer Key

September Matching Game

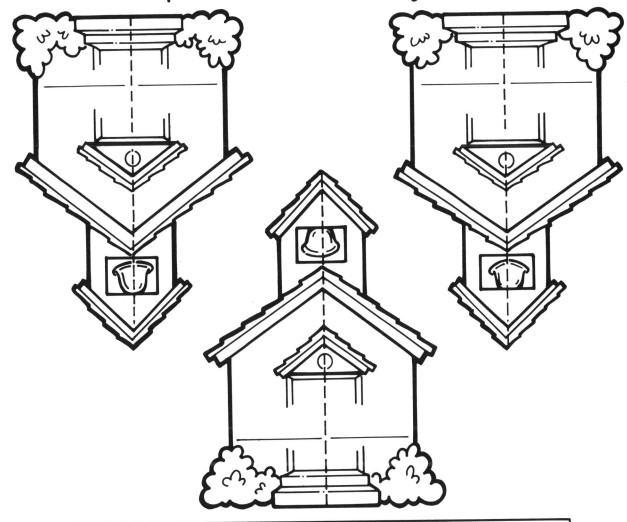

Answer Key

art + room
sticky + glue
lead + pencil
color + crayons
chalk + board
card + catalog
reading + books
writing + stories
social + studies

music + class
physical + education
play + ground
cafeteria + workers
lunch + box
computer + disks
sharp + scissors
safety + patrol

OCTOBER—PUMPKIN PATCH

Theme Decorations   Scarecrow in a field

Materials for the game area:

- Basic equipment
- Pumpkin Patch board game, card games, sorting game, and matching game
- Learning Center Skills Games (See Section 5.)
- October vocabulary cards (Use game cards or write underlined words from game cards on index cards.)
- A sign that says "We read with a scarecrow."
- Poster or sign with student directions, "1. Read the October vocabulary cards to a partner. 2. Play a reading game with a partner."

Materials for the scarecrow and field:

- shirt, blue jeans, straw hat, gloves, boots
- small-size Christmas-tree stand or bucket of damp sand

- lightweight broom
- yardstick
- masking tape
- large safety pins
- construction paper and white glue
- one bale of hay (under $5.00 at feed store or garden shop)
- pumpkins (real, plastic, or construction paper)

Scarecrow directions:

1. Invert broom and secure it into the stand. If you are using a Christmas-tree stand, wrap the broomstick with a thick cloth before tightening the screws. This makes the broom handle thicker and prevents slipping.
2. Slip the yardstick through the shirt sleeves. Don't button the shirt.
3. Using masking tape, secure the yardstick horizontally below the broom head. Wrap masking tape around the broom several times. Then hold the yardstick against the tape on the broomstick and wrap the tape diagonally (about 10 times in each direction) around both sticks.
4. Button the shirt, and attach the back of the shirt to the blue jeans with safety pins. (The front of the shirt tail will hang out over the pants.) Stuff the pants into a pair of boots. If you wish, stuff the legs of the blue jeans with crumpled newspaper. Pin the gloves to the shirt cuffs.
5. Stick hay or pine needles around the cuffs and neck, in the boots, etc.
6. Using white glue, apply construction paper eyes, nose, etc., to the broom head. Add a pair of eyeglasses (poke them through the straw).

Theme Set-Up

1. Stand the scarecrow next to the wall (for stability).
2. Place the bale of hay next to the scarecrow.
3. Arrange pumpkins on top of the hay and on the floor near the scarecrow.
4. Post the signs.

Bulletin Boards

See the illustrations on page 66.

Whole-Group Activities

- Learn new vocabulary (pumpkin, Halloween, jack-o'-lantern).
- Create bulletin board using pumpkin activity sheets.

- Cook winter squash.
- Collect pumpkin and winter squash recipes for a class book.
- Dry gourds to make musical instruments or birdhouses.
- Carve a jack-o'-lantern—toast the pumpkin seeds.
- Visit with an area farmer who grows pumpkins, winter squash, or uses a scarecrow.
- Look for pumpkins in literature—Cinderella's coach, "Peter, Peter, Pumpkin Eater," etc.
- Create a class big book about a jack-o'-lantern or scarecrow.
- Bake pumpkin pies.
- Decorate the October calendar.

PUMPKIN PIE RECIPE

Courtesy of Patricia Tolbert

Materials

Plastic sandwich bags (1 per child)
Foil muffin cups (1 per child)
Plastic bowls
Measuring spoons
Egg beaters
Rolling pins
Graham crackers (2 per child)
Milk (½ cup per child)
Cans of pumpkin (1–2 tsp. per child)
Packages of vanilla instant pudding (2 Tbsp. per child)
Sugar (1 tsp. per child)
Margarine (1 Tbsp. per child)
Bag of candied orange slices (1 per child)

Directions

Crust

1. Have each child place 2 graham crackers in a plastic bag.
2. Seal bag and crush crackers into crumbs with a rolling pin.
3. Add 1 tsp. sugar and 1 Tbsp. margarine and mix right in the bag.
4. Press mixture into a foil cup to form the crust.

Filling

1. Measure 2 Tbsp. vanilla pudding into bowl.
2. Add ½ cup cold milk.
3. Mix with beater until pudding starts to thicken.
4. Add 1 to 2 tsp. pumpkin to pudding and stir.
5. Pour into each crust and decorate with candy orange slice.

Content Area Activities

- Grow pumpkin vines from seeds.
- Study the nutrient value of the squash family.
- Research the history of the jack-o'-lantern.
- Study ways that farmers protect crops from birds, rabbits, and other pests.
- Count the ribs in several different sizes of pumpkins. Is the number of ribs the same or different?
- Estimate the number of seeds in a small pumpkin. Then cut the pumpkin and count the seeds.
- After you carve a jack-o'-lantern, count the seeds. Compare with the number of seeds found in the small pumpkin.
- Create cookbooks using pumpkin and squash recipes.
- Estimate the number of pumpkin seeds in a jar.

Theme Center Activities

- Play skill games that reinforce skills being taught in the reading groups.
- Play the Pumpkin Patch board game, card games, matching game, and sorting game.
- Read October vocabulary cards.

October Bulletin Boards

PUMPKIN PATCH PLACES

A place a story occurs is called a <u>setting</u>. What is one of your favorite settings?

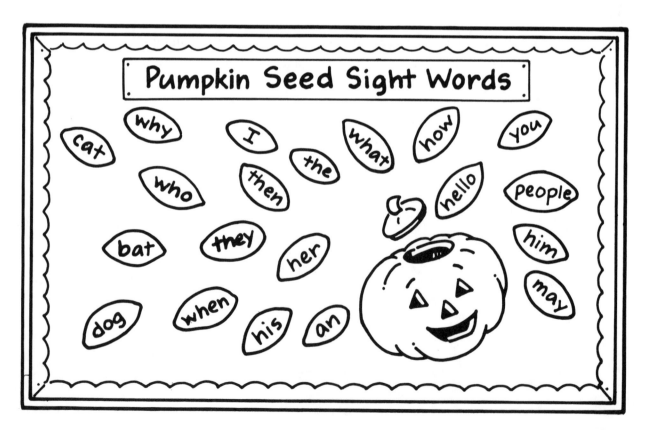

Pumpkin Seed Sight Words

cat why I what how you

who then the hello people

bat they her him

dog when his an may

OCTOBER

SUNDAY	MONDAY	TUESDAY	WEDNESDAY	THURSDAY	FRIDAY	SATURDAY

START

Here comes a ghost!

Move ahead two spaces.

BOO!

Miss a turn.

Game Cards

Trick or Treat! Take one more turn.

Black cat!

Go back one space.

Move ahead one.

P

Go back one space and eat pumpkin pie.

Ride a witch's broom! Move ahead two.

UMPKIN PATCH

You made it through the haunted house. Move ahead one.

FINISH

You Win!

See the scary haunted house.

Pick up acorns.

Eat candy corn.

I drink warm cocoa.

See the orange pumpkin.

Pet a big black cat.

Eat a big red apple.

Wear a Halloween mask.

Sit by a haystack.

See the moon?

See the witch's broomstick.

The ghost says BOO!

Eat candy treats.

TRICK OR TREAT

Wear your warm mittens.

Look at a scary hat.

70

See the
jack-ð-lantern.

I ate the
candied apple.

I can carve
a pumpkin.

I drink
apple cider.

We can rake
the fall leaves.

I like to wear
a costume.

Don't forget to
put on a jacket.

See the
scarecrow.

We celebrate
Columbus Day.

Please wear
your cap.

Build a fire.

Smile!

Listen to the
blackbird.

I like to see
the red leaves.

See the
spider?

October Sorting Game

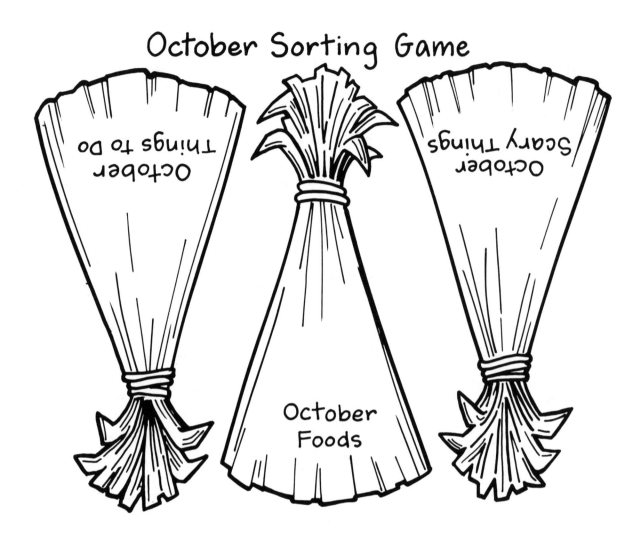

October Things to Do

October Foods

October Scary Things

<u>October <u>Things</u> <u>to</u> <u>Do</u></u>

carve a pumpkin
rake fall leaves
put on a jacket
wear your cap
build a fire
Smile!
see the red leaves
pick up acorns
see the moon
sit by a haystack
listen to the blackbird
celebrate Columbus Day
wear your warm mittens

<u>October <u>Foods</u></u>

candied apple
apple cider
orange pumpkin
cocoa
candy corn
red apple
candy treats

<u>Answer Key</u>

<u>October <u>Scary</u> <u>Things</u></u>

jack-o-lantern
costume
scarecrow
spider
haunted house
Halloween mask
big black cat
scary hat
Boo!
witch's broomstick

October Matching Game

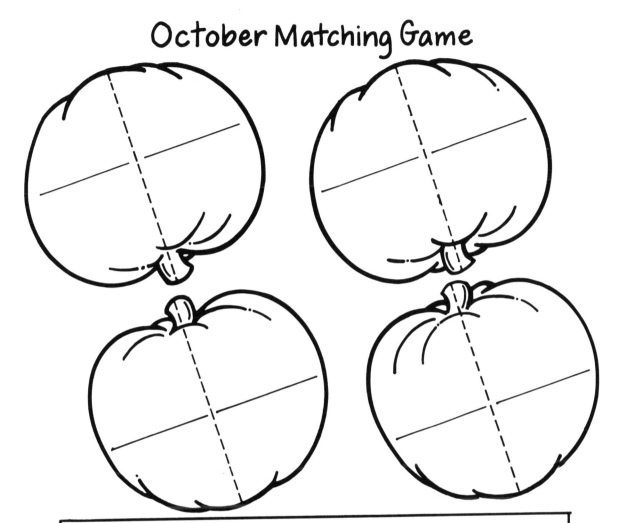

Answer Key

haunted + house
hay + stack
apple + cider
Happy + Halloween
witch's + broomstick
trick + or treat
Columbus + Day
black + cat
scare + crow
pumpkin + pie

wear + a costume
candied + apples
black + bird
rake + leaves
candy + corn
jack + o-lantern
warm + jackets
hot + cocoa
Halloween + mask
red + apple

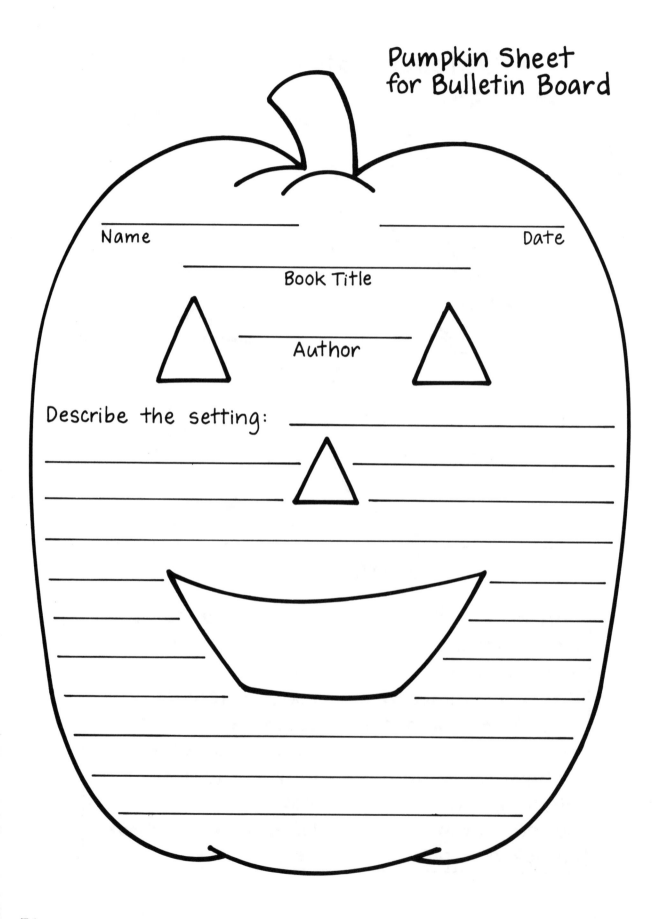

Pumpkin Sheet
for Bulletin Board

Name _____   _____ Date

_____
Book Title

_____
Author

Describe the setting: _____
_____
_____
_____
_____
_____
_____
_____
_____
_____
_____
_____

NOVEMBER—INDIAN TEPEE

Theme Decorations   Indian Tepee

Pattern courtesy of Diane Holman

YOU WILL NEED—

- 8 – 1" X 3" BOARDS:
  4 – 6' AND 4 – 4'
- 2 – ROLLS BROWN WRAPPING
  PAPER OR BUTCHER PAPER
- STRONG THIN ROPE
- ELECTRIC DRILL WITH 3/4" BIT
- COLORED MARKERS

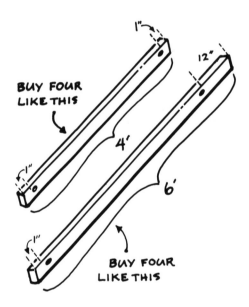

- TIE THE TEPEE TOGETHER, STARTING WITH THE TOP OF THE 6' POLES.

- SPREAD THE BOTTOMS OF THE 6' POLES APART AND TIE A 4' POLE BETWEEN EACH.

- COVER WITH PAPER AND DECORATE.

Materials for the game area:

- Basic equipment
- Indian Tepee board game, card games, sorting game, and matching game
- Learning Center Skills Games (See Section 5)
- November vocabulary cards (Use game cards or write underlined words from game cards on index cards)
- "Indian Partners" chart—a list of student partners and the date they will play reading games in the tepee
- Poster or sign with student directions, "1. Read the November vocabulary cards to a partner. 2. Play a reading game."

For the tepee:

See the directions and illustrations given under "Theme Decorations." If electric drills are foreign to you, ask a handy friend to help. NOTE: To store the tepee, remove the paper, untie the bottom sections, and fold up the poles.

Theme Set-Up

1. Arrange student seating.
2. Set the tepee near the student seating.
3. Post objective, student directions, and Indian Partners chart.

Bulletin Boards

See the illustrations on page 80.

Whole-Group Activities

- Learn new vocabulary (Pilgrim, Indian, tepee, Thanksgiving).
- Learn simple Native American words.
- Role-play the Thanksgiving story.
- Make cranberry sauce on a hot plate. Combine 4 C. fresh cranberries, 2 C. sugar, and 2 C. water. Boil until skins of berries pop (5 min.). Cool and serve in tiny paper cups.
- Visit a turkey farm.
- Create a Thanksgiving song. Write the words on your song chart.
- Make totem poles. (See activity sheet.)
- Glue Indian symbols (on activity sheet) to small magnets. Children can tell stories by moving magnets on metal trays or cookie sheets.

- Conduct Indian/Pilgrim relay races.
- Decorate the November calendar.

Content Area Activities

- Learn the Thanksgiving story.
- Using an encyclopedia, find the route of the Pilgrims.
- Estimate the number of cranberries in a cellophane package. Then count them.
- Gather information about children's favorite Thanksgiving foods. Use the results to create a graph.
- Learn about different Native American tribes.
- Create a Thanksgiving menu.

Theme Center Activities

- Sit in the tepee to play November reading games.
- Play skill games that reinforce skills being taught in the reading groups.
- Play the Indian Tepee board game, card games, matching game, and sorting game.
- Read the November vocabulary cards.

November Bulletin Boards

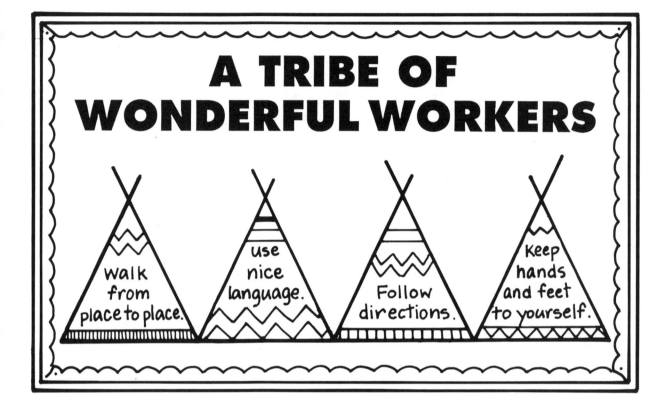

A TRIBE OF WONDERFUL WORKERS

walk from place to place.

use nice language.

Follow directions.

Keep hands and feet to yourself.

A CORNUCOPIA OF SUPER WORKERS

NOVEMBER

SUNDAY	MONDAY	TUESDAY	WEDNESDAY	THURSDAY	FRIDAY	SATURDAY

START

Dinner with a Pilgrim! Move ahead 2.

TAKE A TRIP
ON THE
TEPEE TRAIL

You Win!
FINISH

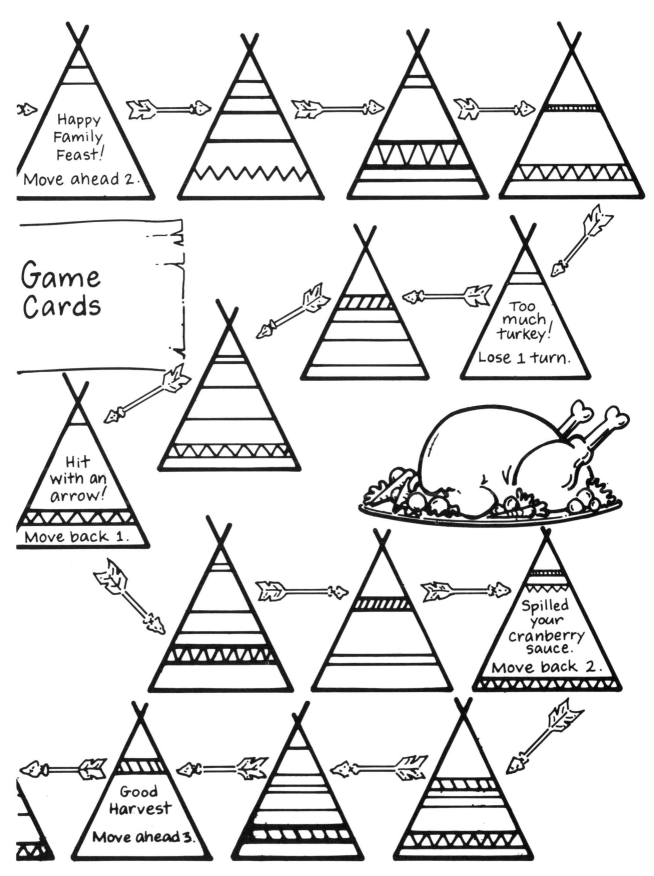

Game Cards

Happy Family Feast! Move ahead 2.

Too much turkey! Lose 1 turn.

Hit with an arrow! Move back 1.

Spilled your cranberry sauce. Move back 2.

Good Harvest Move ahead 3.

A holiday festival is special.

Look at the tepee.

November is a month.

We show our gratitude by saying "Thanks."

We watch football.

The stuffing tastes good.

We eat with our family.

Look at the parade.

The acorn fell from the tree.

The feather headdress is beautiful.

An Indian who helped the Pilgrims was Samoset.

The Pilgrims and Indians smoked a peace pipe.

Squanto was an Indian boy.

The Pilgrims sailed on the Mayflower.

Massasoit was an Indian chief.

Settlers landed on Plymouth Rock.

A totem pole reminds us of Indians.

Thanksgiving is on the third Thursday in November.

Look at the cornucopia of fruit.

The corn husks are pretty.

The autumn season is also called fall.

Eat a yummy turkey dinner.

Look at the colored leaves.

We eat pumpkin pie.

Eat the cranberry sauce.

Indians used a bow and arrow.

The Pilgrims and Indians celebrated.

It is harvest time.

We eat turkey on Thanksgiving Day.

Candied yams taste good.

November Sorting Game

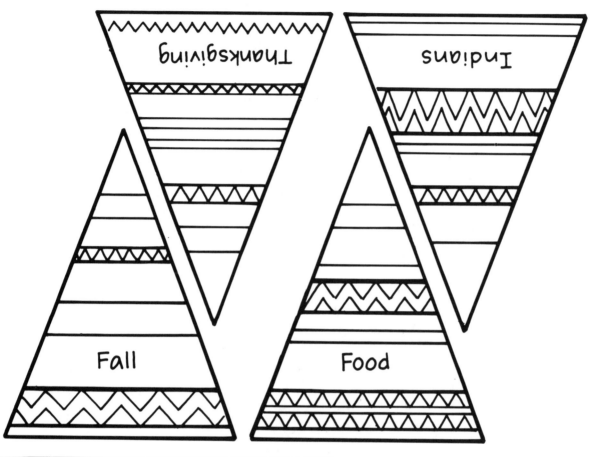

Thanksgiving

Indians

Fall

Food

Answer Key

Indians
bow and arrow
totem pole
tepee
Samoset
peace pipe
Squanto
Massasoit
feather
  headdress

Fall
harvest time
colored leaves
corn husks
autumn season
November
acorn
football
Cornucopia
  of fruit

Thanksgiving
Plymouth Rock
third Thursday
holiday festival
gratitude
family
parade
Mayflower
Thanksgiving Day
Pilgrims and
  Indians

Food
pumpkin pie
candied yams
turkey dinner
stuffing
cranberry
  sauce

November Matching Game

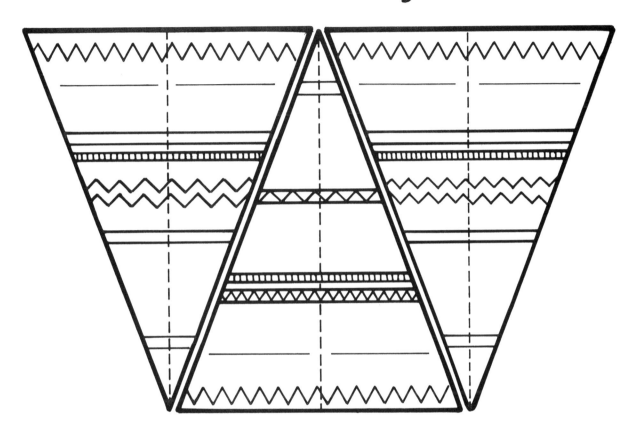

Answer Key

harvest + time	totem + pole
cranberry + sauce	candied + yams
turkey + dinner	peace + pipe
cornucopia + of fruit	pumpkin + pie
Plymouth + Rock	autumn + season
Thanksgiving + Day	third + Thursday
bow + and arrow	holiday + festival
colored + leaves	feather + headdress
corn + husks	Pilgrims + and Indians

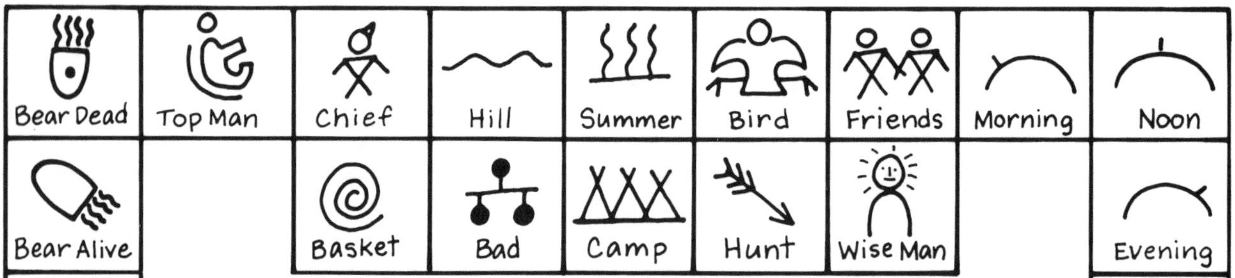

Bear Dead	Top Man	Chief	Hill	Summer	Bird	Friends	Morning	Noon
Bear Alive		Basket	Bad	Camp	Hunt	Wise Man		Evening

Let's Make A Totem Pole!

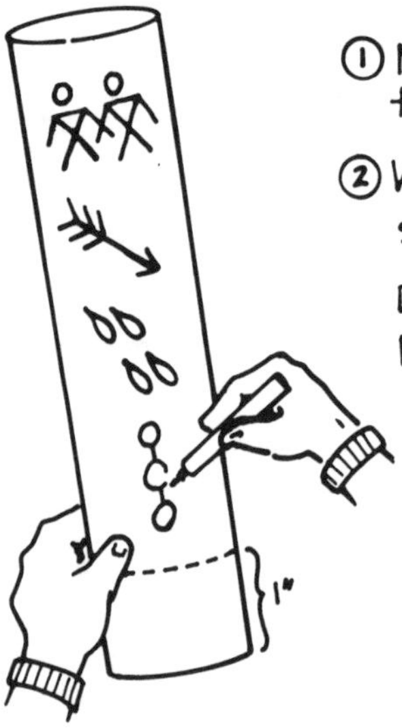

① Make up a story using these Indian symbols.

② Write or paint your symbol story on a paper towel roll.
–or–
Draw symbols on paper and paste on the roll.

③ Leave about one inch empty at the bottom to make the base of your totem pole.

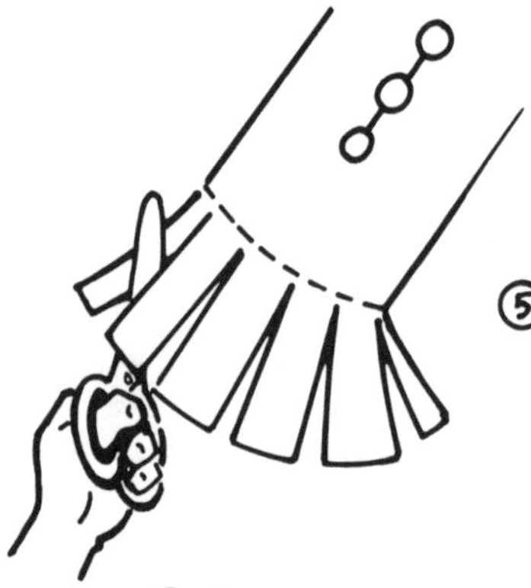

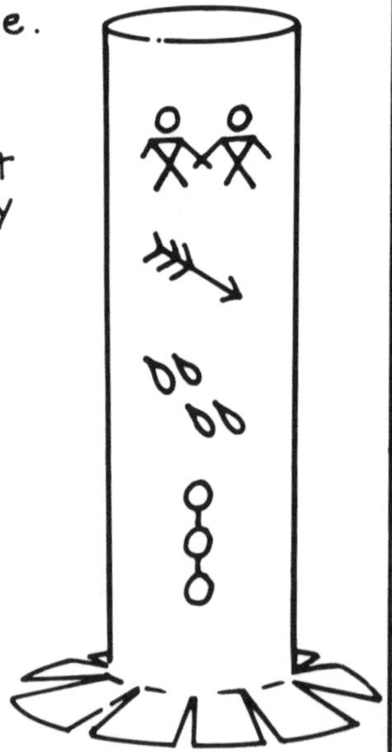

④ Cut the part you left empty at the bottom into wide strips.

⑤ Bend the strips outward to make the base of the totem pole.

⑥ Stand up your totem pole!

Left column symbols:
- Big Voice
- Campfire
- Look
- Fear
- Hungry
- 3 Nights
- 3 Days
- Beaver
- Deer

Right column symbols:
- Directions
- Horses
- Man
- Woman
- Boy
- Man on Horse
- River
- Tepee
- Hear

Middle bottom row: War | Clouds | Brothers | Talk | Make peace

Bottom row: Cold,Snow | Rain | Clear | Stormy | Food | Lake | Eat | Birds | Spirit

DECEMBER/JANUARY—WINTER WONDERLAND

Theme Decorations   Winter snow scene

Materials for the game area:

- Basic equipment
- Winter Wonderland board game, card games, sorting game, and matching game
- Learning Center Skills Games (See Section 5.)
- Winter vocabulary cards (Use game cards or write underlined words from game cards on index cards.)
- A sign that says "Winter is a great time to read!"
- Poster or sign with student directions, "1. Read the winter vocabulary cards. 2. Play a reading game."

For the snow scene:

- Wall space
- Solid-color sheet, blue or white
- Winter pond made of light blue or white construction paper
- White cotton batting and glitter or artificial snow spray
- Christmas lights (optional)
- Hand-drawn ice skaters, evergreens, and snowmen (and women) made by children
- Thumb tacks and straight pins
- Bare branches planted in clay flower pots
- White or light blue snowflake cutouts as described here

Snowflake Directions

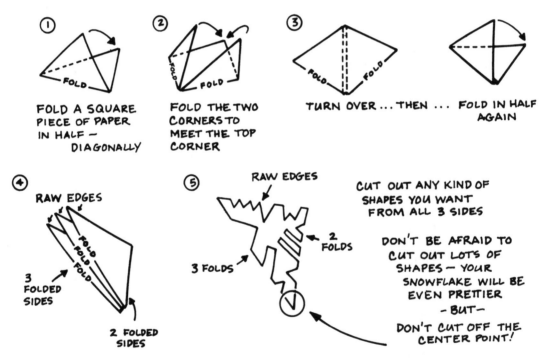

① FOLD A SQUARE PIECE OF PAPER IN HALF — DIAGONALLY

② FOLD THE TWO CORNERS TO MEET THE TOP CORNER

③ TURN OVER ... THEN ... FOLD IN HALF AGAIN

④ RAW EDGES
3 FOLDED SIDES
2 FOLDED SIDES

⑤ RAW EDGES
3 FOLDS
2 FOLDS

CUT OUT ANY KIND OF SHAPES YOU WANT FROM ALL 3 SIDES

DON'T BE AFRAID TO CUT OUT LOTS OF SHAPES — YOUR SNOWFLAKE WILL BE EVEN PRETTIER
— BUT —
DON'T CUT OFF THE CENTER POINT!

⑥ UNFOLD GENTLY AND FLATTEN IN A THICK BOOK FOR A DAY OR SO

⑦ HANG YOUR SNOWFLAKES FROM THE CEILING WITH WHITE THREAD AND TAPE — OR — STICK THEM TO THE WINDOW FOR AN INSTANT SNOW SCENE!

Theme Set-Up

1. Using thumbtacks, hang the sheet on the wall.
2. Tack or pin the cotton batting on the bottom half of the sheet. Sprinkle with glitter or spray with snow.
3. Attach the pond and cutouts to the sheet with straight pins.
4. Stand the pots of bare branches on each side of the scene. Wrap lights around the bare branches.
5. Post the objective and student directions.

Bulletin Boards

See the illustrations on page 93.

Whole-Group Activities

- Learn new vocabulary (snowflake, migrate, hibernate, etc.).
- Role-play holiday stories.
- Bake holiday cookies using a cookie mix and toaster oven.
- Collect holiday canned items for a needy family.
- Make a winter bird feeder for the playground.
- Make hot apple cider—in a crock pot, heat apple cider and 2–3 cinnamon sticks.
- Make snowstorm jars as shown in the illustration.
- Decorate the December and January calendars.

Snowstorm Jars

YOU WILL NEED—
- 1 SMALL JAR WITH A TIGHT LID
- 1 SMALL PLASTIC FORM SUCH AS A SNOWMAN
- HOT GLUE GUN, GLUE OR FLORAL CLAY
- SILVER GLITTER
- LIQUID DETERGENT
- WATER

DIRECTIONS—

1. USING THE HOT GLUE GUN (OR GLUE OR FLORAL CLAY) STICK THE PLASTIC FORM TO THE JAR LID.

2. PUT ONE TEASPOON OF GLITTER IN THE JAR AND SLOWLY FILL WITH WATER. ADD ONE DROP OF DETERGENT.

3. SCREW THE LID TIGHT, INVERT THE JAR AND SHAKE GENTLY TO MAKE A SNOWSTORM.

Content Area Activities

- Study how snowflakes are made and why each is different.
- Using an encyclopedia, find out how igloos are made.
- Keep a daily record of high and low temperatures.
- Create an illustrated timeline of winter holidays—Hanukkah, Christmas, New Year's Day, Martin Luther King Day.
- Learn about winter animal habits—migration, hibernation, etc.
- Find out how evergreens differ from deciduous plants and trees.
- Set up filmstrip viewers with filmstrips—Dr. Martin Luther King, holidays, winter animals, and evergreens.

Theme Center Activities

- Play skill games that reinforce skills being taught in the reading groups.
- Play the Winter Wonderland board game, card games, matching game, and sorting game.
- Read winter vocabulary cards.

December/January Bulletin Boards

WONDERFUL
WINTER
WORDS

star
holiday   snow
icy   cold   Santa
snowman   give   presents   elf

fire   presents
stocking
skiing
sled

'Tis the Season for Lots of READING

Mark   Sue   Kay   Tom   Alan   Nancy   Janet

BOOK REPORT (on each stocking)

DECEMBER

SUNDAY	MONDAY	TUESDAY	WEDNESDAY	THURSDAY	FRIDAY	SATURDAY

JANUARY

SUNDAY	MONDAY	TUESDAY	WEDNESDAY	THURSDAY	FRIDAY	SATURDAY

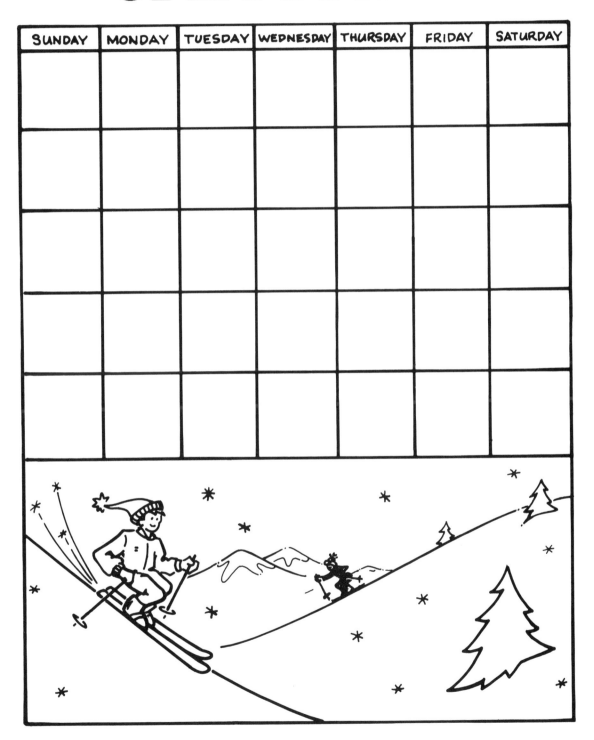

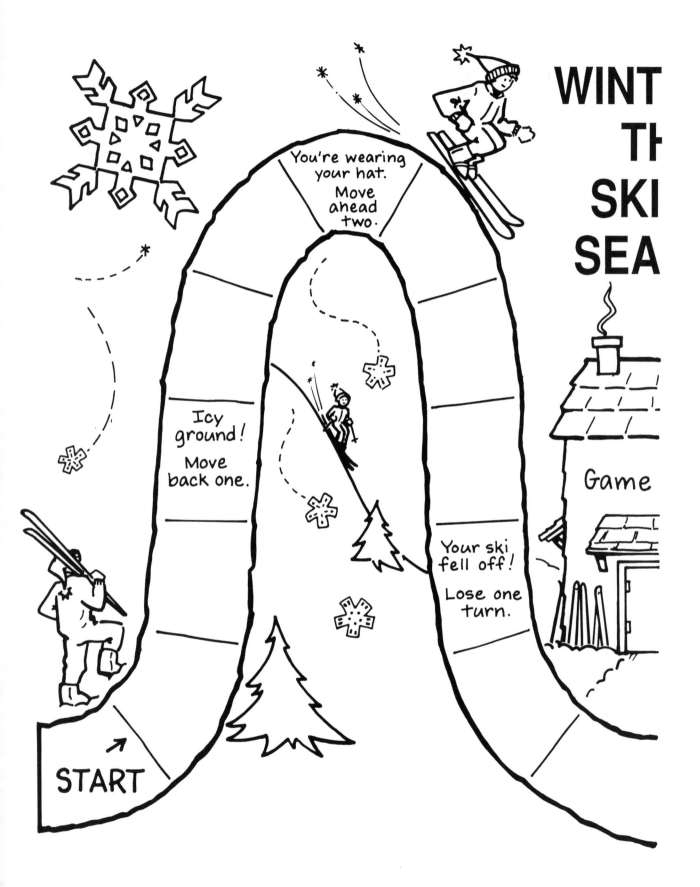

WINT
Tl
SKI
SEA

You're wearing
your hat.
Move
ahead
two.

Icy
ground!
Move
back one.

Your ski
fell off!
Lose one
turn.

Game

START

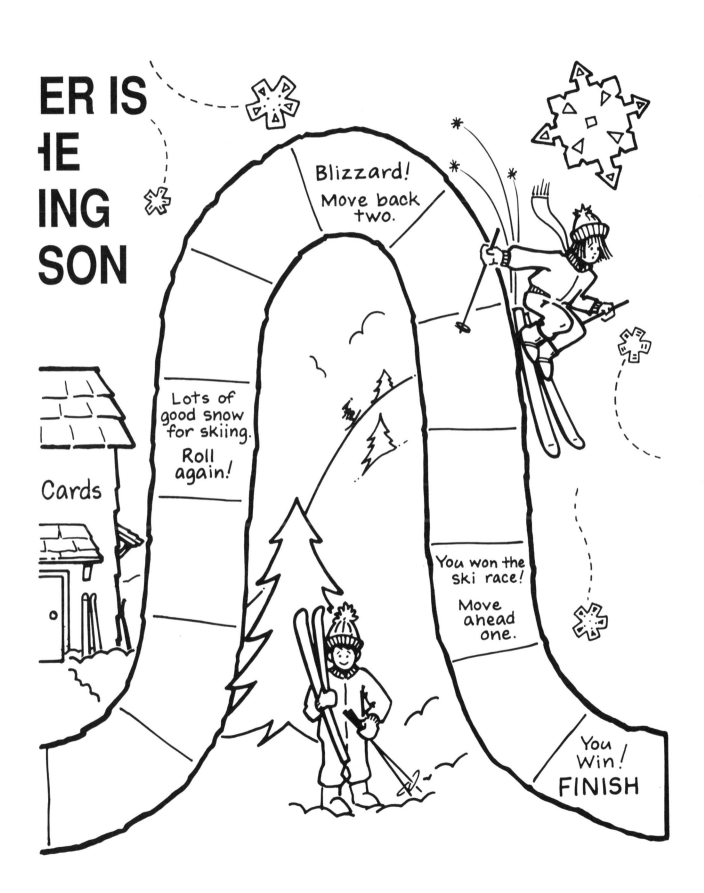

ER IS
HE
ING
SON

Cards

Blizzard!
Move back
two.

Lots of
good snow
for skiing.
Roll
again!

You won the
ski race!

Move
ahead
one.

You
Win!
FINISH

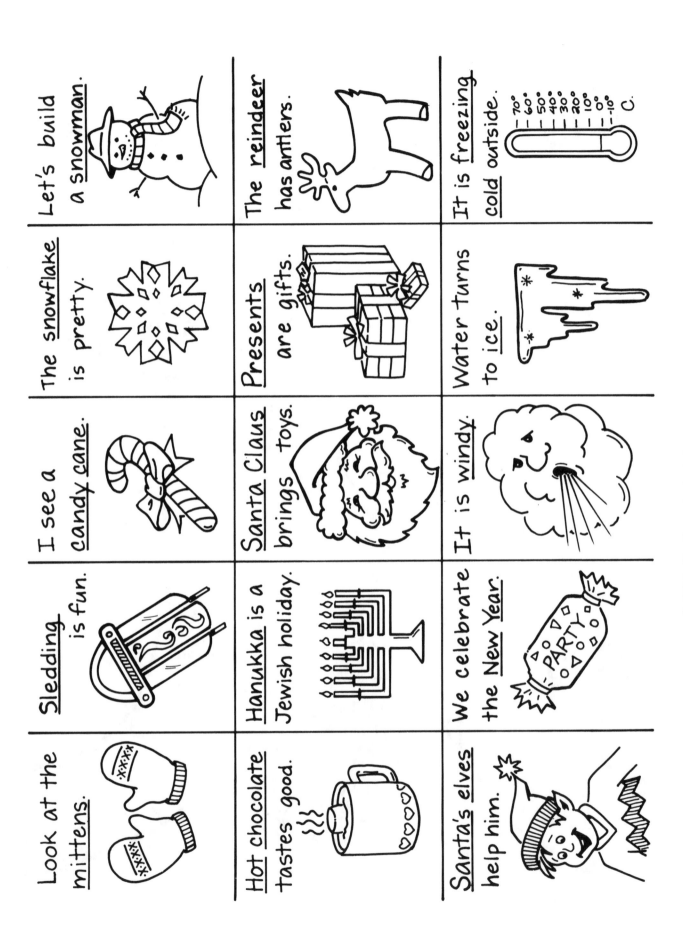

Let's build a snowman.

The reindeer has antlers.

It is freezing cold outside.

The snowflake is pretty.

Presents are gifts.

Water turns to ice.

I see a candy cane.

Santa Claus brings toys.

It is windy.

Sledding is fun.

Hanukka is a Jewish holiday.

We celebrate the New Year.

Look at the mittens.

Hot chocolate tastes good.

Santa's elves help him.

See the mistletoe.

The holly wreath is pretty.

Ornaments are decorations.

Look at the boots.

Ice skating is fun.

Let's sit by the fireplace.

Look at the wool scarf.

See the winter coat.

This is a hat.

Look at the Christmas tree.

Ice hockey is a sport.

The sweater is warm.

Ride on the snowmobile!

Stockings are warm.

Downhill skiing is fun.

December/January Sorting Game

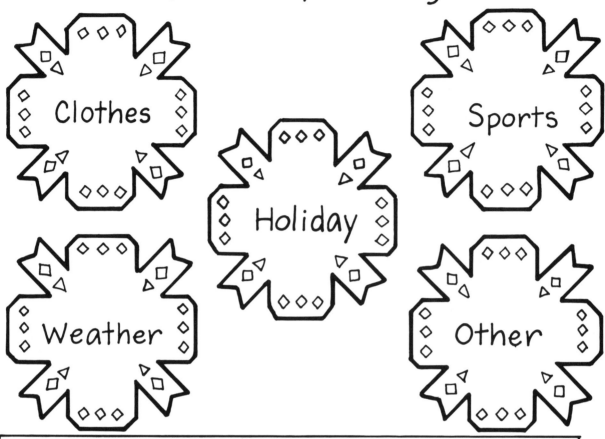

Clothes

Sports

Holiday

Weather

Other

Answer Key

Holiday	Clothes	Sports
Christmas tree	stockings	ice hockey
presents	mittens	downhill skiing
Santa Claus	winter coat	ice skating
Hanukka	hat	sledding
Santa's elves	wool scarf	snowmobile
reindeer	boots	**Weather**
New Year	sweater	snowflake
candy cane	**Other**	ice
mistletoe	hot chocolate	freezing cold
ornaments	snowman	windy
holly wreath	fireplace	

December / January Matching Game

Answer Key

downhill + skiing	wool + scarf
ice + skating	winter + coat
Christmas + tree	New + Year
Santa + Claus	candy + cane
freezing + cold	holly + wreath
snow + flake	hot + chocolate
Santa's + elves	snow + man
rein + deer	snow + mobile
ice + hockey	fire + place

FEBRUARY—ST. VALENTINE'S DAY AND DENTAL HEALTH MONTH

Theme Decorations   Post Office

Materials for the game area:

- Basic equipment
- Valentine board game, card games, sorting game, and matching game
- Learning Center Skills Games (See Section 5.)
- February vocabulary cards (Use game cards or write underlined words from game cards on index cards.)
- Dental-health posters, purchased or made by the children
- A sign that says "Post office messages are fun to read."
- Poster or sign with student directions, "1. Read the February vocabulary cards to a partner. 2. Play a reading game."

For the mailbox:

- Cardboard box, about 18 inches square
- Pink and red construction paper
- Lace doilies
- Tape and glue
- Scissors

Directions for the box:

1. Cut the flaps from the top of the box. Turn the box over.
2. Cut a slit in what is now the top.
3. Cover the cardboard by taping pink or red (or both) construction paper to the box.

Directions for the decorations:

1. Show children how to make a heart by folding a square of paper and drawing half a heart shape. Remind them to draw the heart "out" from the fold.
2. Distribute squares of construction paper and lace doilies.
3. Have the children make and decorate hearts any size they wish.
4. When the hearts are finished, have children glue their hearts on the box.

Theme Set-Up

1. Set the mailbox on a table or shelf in the Theme Center.
2. Hang dental-health posters on the wall near the mailbox. Arrange student seating nearby.
3. Post objective and student directions.

Bulletin Boards

See the illustrations on page 105.

Whole-Group Activities

- Learn new vocabulary (Valentine, post office, toothbrush, dental care, flossing, brushing, etc.).
- Create the Valentine mailbox.
- Visit a post office.
- Choose pen pals from another classroom. Exchange Valentine messages.

- Create a Valentine song to write on the song chart. Record the class singing it.
- Invite a dentist to speak to the class.
- Create a class song about dental care to add to the song chart.
- Decorate the February calendar.

Content Area Activities

- Study the lives of George Washington and Abraham Lincoln.
- Brainstorm and develop two lists—one with foods which promote good teeth and one with foods that are harmful to teeth.
- Estimate the number of (wrapped) Valentine candies in a package, count them, then eat them.
- Celebrate President's Day.
- Bake cherry pies in a toaster oven. Fill store-bought tart shells with canned cherry pie filling. Follow baking directions on the tart-shell package. Cool, garnish with whipped topping, and serve.

Theme Center Activities

- Play skill games that reinforce skills being taught in the reading groups.
- Play the Valentine board game, card games, sorting game, and matching game.
- Read February vocabulary cards.

February Bulletin Boards

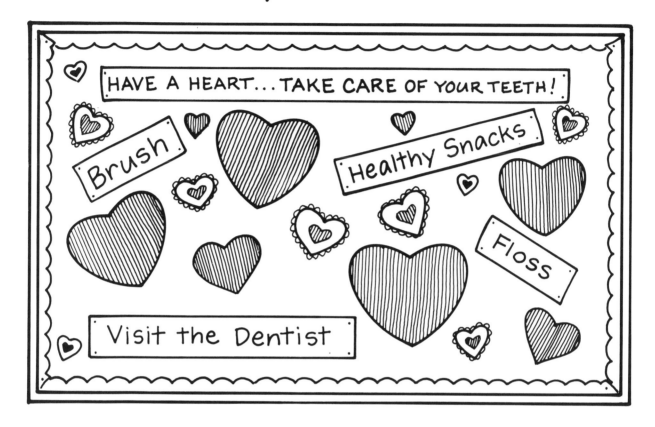

HAVE A HEART... TAKE CARE OF YOUR TEETH!

Brush

Healthy Snacks

Floss

Visit the Dentist

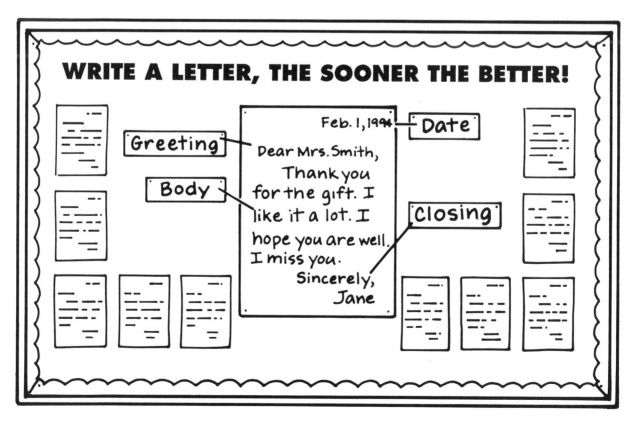

WRITE A LETTER, THE SOONER THE BETTER!

Date

Feb. 1, 1994

Greeting

Dear Mrs. Smith,
   Thank you for the gift. I like it a lot. I hope you are well. I miss you.

Body

Closing

Sincerely,
      Jane

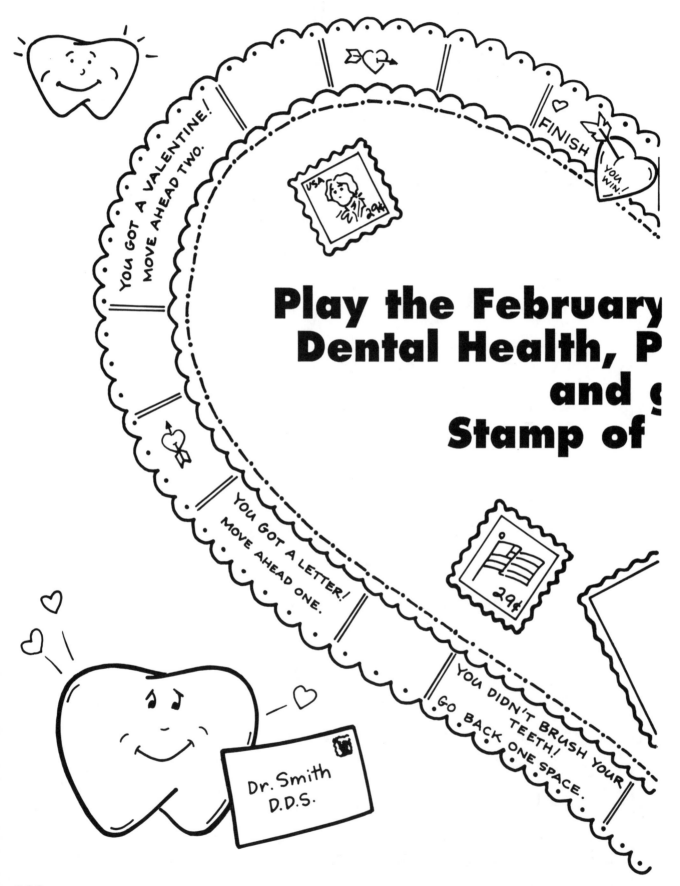

Play the February
Dental Health, P
and
Stamp of

YOU GOT A VALENTINE!
MOVE AHEAD TWO.

FINISH
YOU WIN!

YOU GOT A LETTER!
MOVE AHEAD ONE.

YOU DIDN'T BRUSH YOUR TEETH!
GO BACK ONE SPACE.

USA 29¢

29¢

Dr. Smith
D.D.S.

START

NO CAVITIES! ROLL AGAIN!

DENTAL HEALTH

y Valentine's Day,
ost Office Game
get a
Approval!

GAME CARDS

FORGOT TO MAIL YOUR VALENTINE! LOSE ONE TURN.

Look at the mailbox.

See the letter.

The envelope is white.

The heart is a symbol.

A red rose is a symbol of love.

Valentine's Day is on February 14th.

See the Valentine card.

Put the zip code on my letter.

Cupid is an angel.

We show love on Valentine's Day.

Look at the box of chocolate candy.

Cupid shoots a bow and arrow.

The package was delivered.

Put a stamp on the letter.

Do you know your address?

Mr. Joe Smith
5 Red Street
Miami, FL 33192

The delivery truck is here.	Put the <u>return</u> address on the letter.	The <u>postcard</u> is small.	The <u>mail carrier</u> is friendly.	Make sure to <u>floss</u>.
Brushing <u>teeth</u> is important.	Healthy <u>snacks</u> are important.	<u>Toothpaste</u> should be used.	<u>Metal braces</u> straighten teeth.	The <u>dentist's</u> office is busy.
A <u>cavity</u> hurts.	<u>Mouthwash</u> is useful.	Everyone likes <u>kisses and hugs</u>. S.W.A.K.	<u>Junk food</u> is unhealthy.	Fight <u>tooth decay</u>.

Dear Sue,
How are
you? I am
fine.
Love,
Jim

C. Smith
5 Red St.
Miami, FL
32508

U.S. MAIL

Dr. Smith
D.D.S.
WALK IN

DENTAL HEALTH AWARD

TOOTHPASTE

MOUTH WASH

February Sorting Game

Valentine's Day

POST OFFICE

Dental Health

Answer Key

Valentine's Day	Post Office	Dental Health
heart	mail carrier	healthy snacks
Cupid	envelope	floss
love	letter	toothpaste
chocolate candy	package	brushing teeth
bow and arrow	stamp	metal braces
February 14th	address	dentist's office
red rose	zip code	cavity
valentine card	return address	mouthwash
kisses and hugs	delivery truck	junk food
	post card	tooth decay
	mail box	

February Matching Game

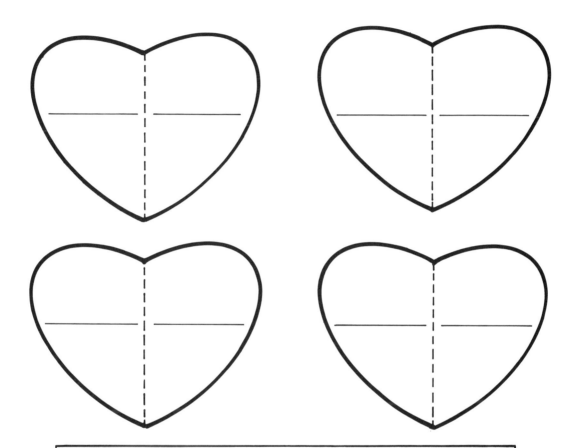

Answer Key

mail + carrier   post + card
zip + code   mail + box
return + address   healthy + snacks
chocolate + candy   tooth + decay
bow + arrow   tooth + paste
February + 14th   brushing + teeth
red + rose   mouth + wash
valentine + card   dentist's + office
kisses + hugs   metal + braces
delivery + truck

FEBRUARY

SUNDAY	MONDAY	TUESDAY	WEDNESDAY	THURSDAY	FRIDAY	SATURDAY

MARCH—SPACE SHIP

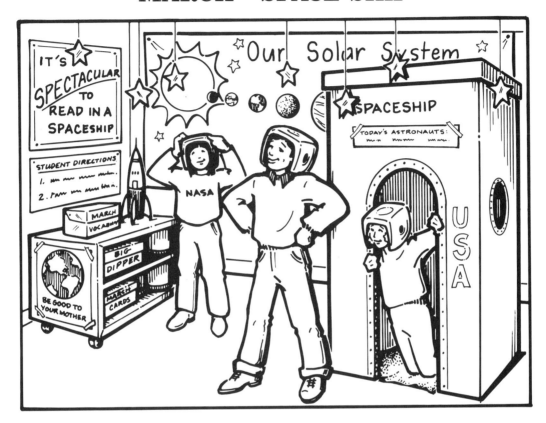

Theme Decorations   Space ship

Materials for the game area:

- Basic equipment
- Space ship board game, card games, sorting game, and matching game
- Learning Center Skills Games (See Section 5.)
- March vocabulary cards (Use game cards or write underlined words from game cards on index cards.)
- List of children who will sit in the space ship each day.
- A sign that says "It's spectacular to read in a space ship."
- Poster or sign with student directions, "1. Read the Space Ship vocabulary cards to a partner. 2. Play a reading game."

Materials for the space ship:

- Appliance box with top
- Silver spray paint
- Throw rug

Theme Set-Up

1. Let the children paint a mural of the solar system. Hang it on a wall in the theme center.
2. Spray paint the appliance box and box top. Stand the box upright and use a sharp knife or safety razor blade to cut a door tall enough for children to see out when they sit in the box. Place the throw rug in the bottom.

Bulletin Boards

See the illustrations on page 116.

Whole-Group Activities

- Learn new vocabulary (planet, galaxy, space capsule, etc.).
- Build models of the moon and planets.
- Make space helmets.

   Plastic gallon milk jugs—Cut the top off the jug, cut an arch in one side for the face, and spray silver or cover with foil.

   Grocery bags—In the front of the bag cut a hole for the face. Decorate with paint and foil.
- Create a mural of the solar system for the theme set up.
- Make a class book of astronauts—make a snapshot of each child sitting in the spaceship. Have the children write stories about their "spaceship ride." Glue the children's pictures to their stories and bind together for a class book.
- Make Zero-Gravity Space Pudding.
- Decorate the March calendar.

ZERO GRAVITY SPACE PUDDING RECIPE

Courtesy of Diane Holman

Materials:

1 small self-sealing plastic bag for each child
Instant pudding and milk

Directions:

1. Put 1 T. instant pudding and ¼ C. milk in each bag. Zip bag closed.
2. Squeeze the bag to make pudding. Let it stand several minutes.
3. Cut a corner off the bag. Sip the pudding through the hole.

Content Area Activities

- Learn the solar system.
- Study the history of rockets.
- Read about the U.S. space program.
- Learn about the constellations.
- Find longitude and latitude lines on a globe.
- Identify continents and oceans on a map.
- Find out how many miles the earth is from the sun, moon, mars, etc.
- Align planets smallest to largest.
- List which planets have moons and which do not.
- Find the length of day and year on each planet.
- Define meteoroids, asteroids, comets, and galaxies.
- Answer this question. What is an orbit?

Theme Center Activities

- Sit in the space ship to play reading games.
- Play skill games that reinforce skills being taught in the reading groups.
- Play the Space ship board game, card games, sorting game, and matching game.
- Read March vocabulary cards.

March Bulletin Boards

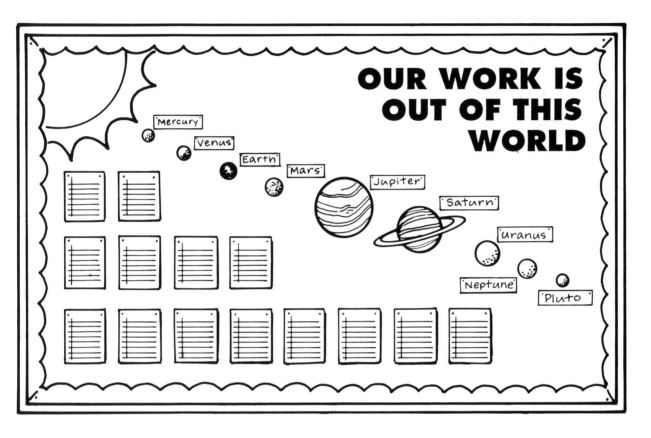

OUR WORK IS OUT OF THIS WORLD

Mercury, Venus, Earth, Mars, Jupiter, Saturn, Uranus, Neptune, Pluto

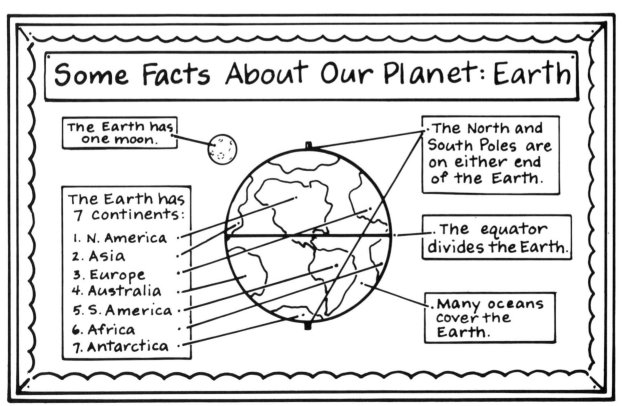

Some Facts About Our Planet: Earth

The Earth has one moon.

The North and South Poles are on either end of the Earth.

The Earth has 7 continents:
1. N. America
2. Asia
3. Europe
4. Australia
5. S. America
6. Africa
7. Antarctica

The equator divides the Earth.

Many oceans cover the Earth.

MARCH

SUNDAY	MONDAY	TUESDAY	WEDNESDAY	THURSDAY	FRIDAY	SATURDAY

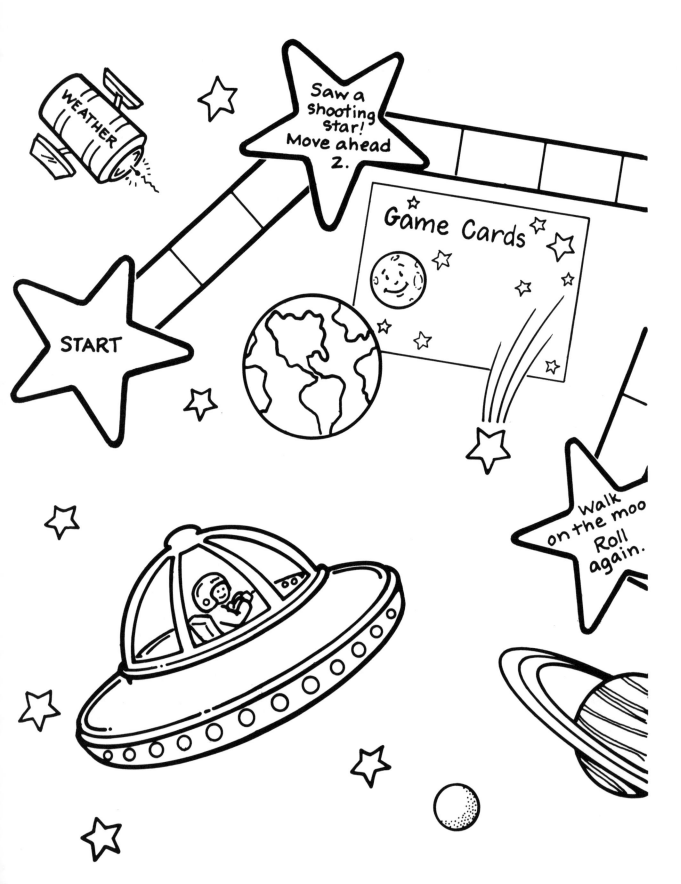

TAKE A TRIP
ON THE
BIG DIPPER

No gravity! Lose 1 turn.

FINISH You Win!

Blast Off! Move ahead 1.

Too far from Earth! Go back 1.

We live in the United States.

Astronauts put satellites in space.

There are no real Martians.

The North and South Poles are on each end of the Earth.

N. Pole

S. Pole

All the planets make up the solar system.

A U.F.O. is pretend.

The equator divides the Earth.

There are many blue oceans.

An alien is not real.

The bright Sun is hot.

There are seven continents.

Cape Canaveral is in Florida.

CAPE CANAVERAL

See the shooting star.

Longitude and latitude lines divide the Earth.

YOU ARE HERE

The rocket will orbit the moon.

120

We live on Earth.

Big Jupiter is a planet.

Venus is a cloudy planet.

Neighborly Mars is close to Earth.

Saturn's rings surround it.

Mercury is close to the Sun.

Tiny Pluto is far away.

Uranus is closer than Neptune.

Neptune is closer than Pluto.

An astronaut explores space.

The spaceship goes fast.

Look through a telescope.

A flying saucer is make-believe.

Constellations are groups of stars.

The Earth has one moon.

March Sorting Game

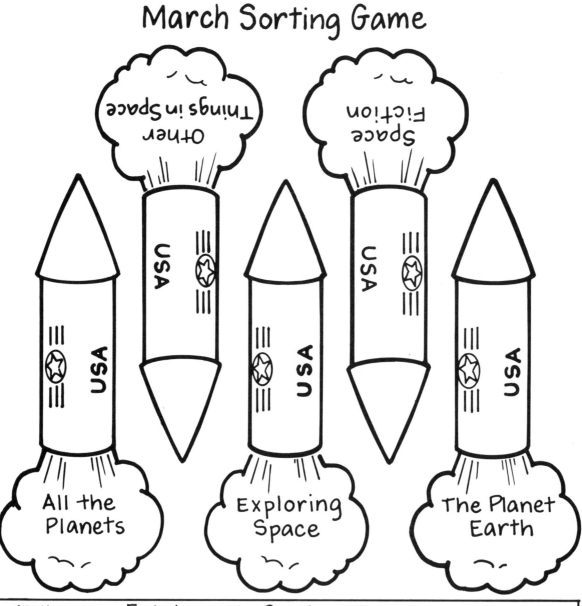

Other Things in Space

Space Fiction

USA

USA

USA

USA

USA

All the Planets

Exploring Space

The Planet Earth

All the Planets	Exploring Space	The Planet Earth	Space Fiction	Other Things in Space
Earth	astronaut	seven continents	alien	constellations
Big Jupiter	Cape Canaveral	blue oceans	flying saucer	moon
Venus	spaceship	United States	Martian	shooting star
Saturn's rings	orbit	equator	U.F.O.	solar system
Mercury	satellite	North/South Pole		bright sun
Tiny Pluto	telescope	longitude and latitude		
Uranus				<u>Answer Key</u>
Neptune				
Neighborly Mars				

March Matching Game

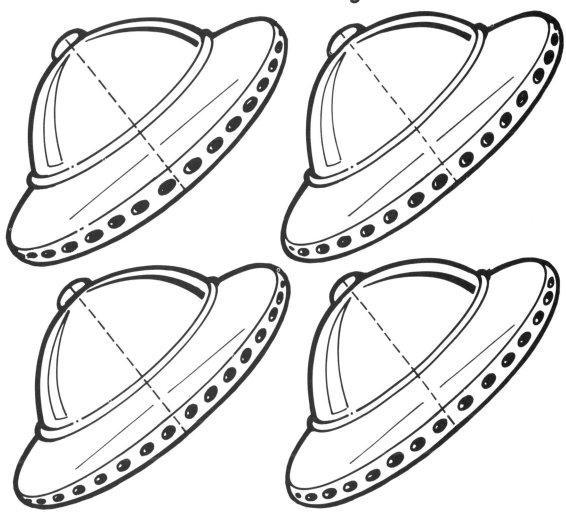

Answer Key

latitude + longitude
space + ship
Saturn's + rings
tiny + Pluto
seven + continents
blue + oceans
United + States

big + Jupiter
solar + system
flying + saucer
North and South + Poles
shooting + star
bright + Sun
neighborly + Mars

APRIL—SPRING TIME

Theme Decorations   Umbrella and flowers

Materials for the game area:

- Basic equipment
- Spring board game, card games, sorting game, and matching game
- Learning Center Skills Games (See Section 5.)
- April vocabulary cards (Use game cards or write underlined words from game cards on index cards.)
- A sign that says "Spring into good reading."
- Poster or sign with student directions, "1. Read the Spring vocabulary cards to a partner. 2. Play a reading game."

Materials for the theme:

- Large umbrella, or several small ones
- Strong cord

Theme Set-Up

1. Tie cord to the point of umbrella(s)
2. Open the umbrella(s) and hang from the ceiling or light fixture.

Bulletin Boards

See the illustrations on page 127.

Whole-Group Activities

- Learn new vocabulary (seeds, blossoms, Earth Day, etc.).
- Celebrate Earth Day.
- Plant a tree in the school yard.
- Make "delicious" bird nests. Decorate cupcakes with green icing, coconut, and jelly beans.
- Dye colored eggs.
- Decorate construction-paper eggs with glitter, yarn, and paint.
- Visit a farm.
- Plant seeds using potting soil and disposable cups.
- Plant dish gardens—Use large plastic butter tubs, potting soil, pebbles, and green plants.
- Make Hairy Harry.
- Decorate the April calendar.

Directions:

1. With markers, draw a face on the side of a disposable cup.
2. Fill cup with potting soil, plant grass seed in the top, and keep moist. When the grass seed sprouts, you will have Hairy Harry.

Content Area Activities

- Keep a log of weather patterns—rain, lightning, thunder, and rainbows.
- Study the life cycles of frogs and butterflies.
- Using a science textbook, conduct a unit on flowers—parts of a flower, and the role of bees and other insects in pollination.
- Plan a garden. Measure length, width, plan number of rows, and decide what flowers and vegetables will be planted in each row.
- Find out why rainbows appear.
- Learn to measure. Use measuring spoons to make egg salad sandwiches.

EGG SALAD SANDWICHES RECIPE

Courtesy of Ardyth Ann Stanley

Materials for each child:

1 disposable cup

1 hard-boiled egg

2 slices bread

Plastic serrated knife

Waxed paper

Mayonnaise, milk, mustard, diced celery or pickle relish

Directions:

Measure 2 tsp. mayonnaise into cup.

Measure ¼ tsp. mustard into cup.

Measure 1 tsp. milk into cup. Stir the mixture.

Crack and peel the egg.

Put the egg on waxed paper. With the knife, cut the egg into small pieces and place in the cup.

Add 1 tsp. celery or pickle relish.

Stir and spread on bread.

Theme Center Activities

- Sit under the umbrella to play reading games.
- Play skill games that reinforce skills being taught in the reading groups.
- Play the Spring Time board game, card games, sorting game, and matching game.
- Read April vocabulary cards.

April Bulletin Boards

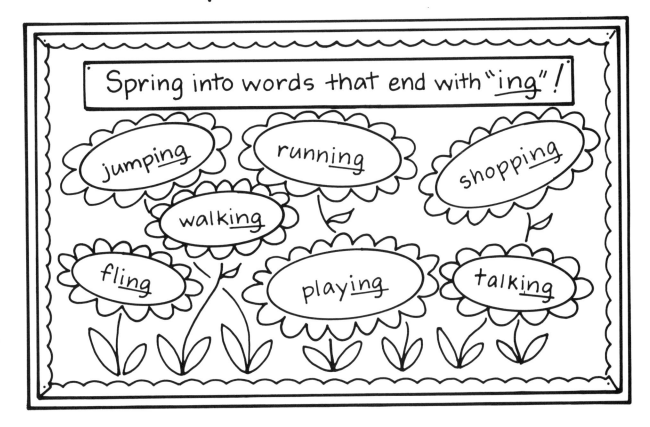

LET'S GO FLOWER HOPPING

START

See a rainbow. Roll again.

Game Cards

Found some Easter eggs. Move ahead one.

Stung by a bee! Lose one turn.

Caught in a thunderstorm. Go back two.

FINISH
You
Win!

Your garden grew.
Move ahead one.

See the rosebud.

Look at the grass.

See the snake.

A rainbow comes at the end of a storm.

See the blossoms.

Jump in the mud puddle.

Thunder and lightning can be scary.

The flower basket is pretty.

The Easter Bunny hops.

HAPPY EASTER!

Put on your hat.

See the green tree.

Seeds grow to be plants.

BEANS

See the drop of rain.

A daisy is pretty.

Plant in the garden.

The buzzing bee flies.

See the basket of goodies.

Look at the storm clouds.

Look at the bunny rabbit.

I like colored eggs.

Wear your rain boots.

Chirping birds sound good.

Look at the duck.

See the umbrella.

The white lamb is soft.

Look at the frog.

I like Earth Day.

See the fluffy chick.

See the butterfly.

Celebrate Arbor Day.

April Sorting Game

Answer Key

Animals	Holiday	Rain Things	Plants & Flowers
fluffy chick	Easter Bunny	drop of rain	rose bud
white lamb	colored eggs	umbrella	daisy
chirping birds	basket of goodies	rain boots	green tree
bunny rabbit	Arbor Day	hat	flower basket
buzzing bee	Earth Day	mud puddle	blossoms
butterfly		storm clouds	grass
frog		rainbow	garden
duck		thunder and	seeds
snake		lightning	

April Matching Game

Answer Key

Chirping + birds
bunny + rabbit
buzzing + bee
butter + fly
drop + of rain
mud + puddles
storm + clouds
thunder + lightning
rain + bow
white + lamb

Easter + bunny
rain + bow
Arbor + Day
colored + eggs
basket + of goodies
Earth + Day
rose + bud
green + tree
flower + basket
fluffy + chick

APRIL

SUNDAY	MONDAY	TUESDAY	WEDNESDAY	THURSDAY	FRIDAY	SATURDAY

MAY—RESTAURANT

Theme Decorations   In a restaurant

Materials for the game area:

- Basic equipment
- Restaurant board game, card games, sorting game, and matching game
- Learning Center Skills Games (See Section 5.)
- May vocabulary cards (Use game cards or write underlined words from game cards on index cards.)
- A sign that says "We read menus and signs in a restaurant."
- Poster or sign with student directions, "1. Read a menu and the May vocabulary cards to a partner. 2. Play a reading game."

For the restaurant:

- Table and chairs for two children
- Tablecloth, or place mats, napkins, centerpiece

- Plastic dinnerware
- Cookware
- Cardboard box (the size of a toy stove)
- Cardboard box (to store other restaurant equipment)
- Serving tray
- Menus
- Aprons
- White paper bag for chef's hat (roll open edges twice to make a cuff)
- Pencils and note pads
- Toy money
- Posters "Help Wanted," "Non-Smoking Area" and "Shoes and Shirts Required."
- Daily list of children to role play

Theme Set-Up

1. Set the table for two with tablecloth, centerpiece, napkins and dinnerware.
2. Using the magic markers, draw burners and an oven door on the cardboard box. Put the chef's hat and cookware on the stove.
3. Store restaurant equipment (menus, aprons, etc.) in the other box.
4. Display restaurant signs.
5. Post objective, list for role play, and student directions.

Bulletin Boards

See the illustrations on page 139.

Whole-Group Activities

- Learn new vocabulary (appetizer, entree, chef).
- Role-play ordering a meal in a restaurant.
- Role-play ordering at a drive-through window.
- Discuss the meanings of signs such as "Help Wanted," "Non-Smoking Area," "Shirt and Shoes Required," "No Pets," etc.
- Display logos (no smoking, men's and women's restrooms, credit cards). Decide where each sign would be found.
- Learn the proper way to set a table.
- Visit the lunchroom while lunch is being prepared.

- Have a chef talk to the class.
- Visit a restaurant and order lunch.
- Collect advertisement cards from supermarket delis. Use them to list foods, list abbreviations, plan a picnic, or arrange in ABC order.
- Create a donut shop. Then list and display words that describe donuts.
- Decorate the May calendar.

THE DONUT SHOP

Courtesy of Ardyth Ann Stanley

Materials:

Small deep fryer and oil
Paper towels
Strainer
Canned biscuits
Canned frosting and powdered sugar

Directions:

1. Heat oil.
2. Poke a finger through the biscuit.
3. Fry the biscuit until brown, 10–15 seconds.
4. Drain on paper towels.
5. Choose frosting or powdered sugar for topping.

Content Area Activities

- Study the food groups.
- Eat foods from other countries.
- Compare the school lunchroom with a local restaurant. How are they alike and different?
- Provide math story problems (Hamburger 80 cents + cheese 10 cents extra = ?).
- Learn about different types of restaurants such as fast food, ethnic, and cafeteria-style.
- Gather information about children's favorite restaurants and graph the results.

- Have children bring in empty food boxes and cans. Use paper bags to sort foods into categories (colors, food groups, beginning sounds, wet versus dry, or breakfast-lunch-dinner-snacks).
- Provide cookbooks for children to copy their favorite recipes.

Theme Center Activities

- Using menus, role play restaurant cook, waiter and waitress, and customer.
- Play skill games that reinforce skills being taught in the reading groups.
- Play the Restaurant board game, card games, sorting game, and matching game.
- Read May vocabulary cards.

May Bulletin Boards

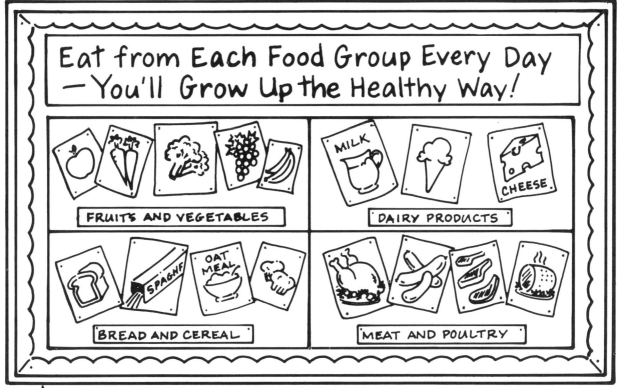

Eat from Each Food Group Every Day —You'll Grow Up the Healthy Way!

FRUITS AND VEGETABLES

DAIRY PRODUCTS

BREAD AND CEREAL

MEAT AND POULTRY

HAVE KIDS CUT OUT MAGAZINE PICTURES OF FOOD TO PUT IN EACH FOOD GROUP

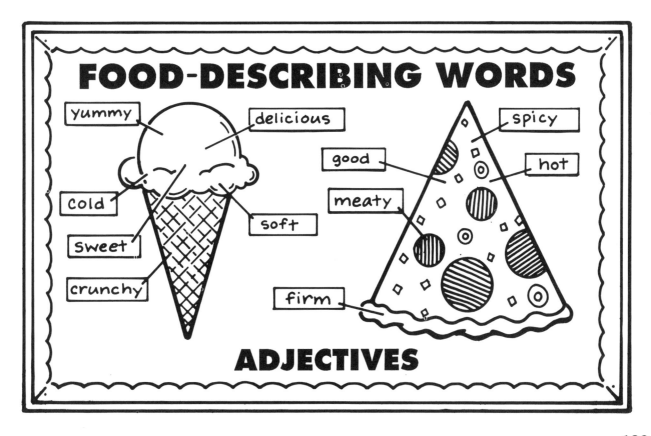

FOOD-DESCRIBING WORDS

yummy

delicious

spicy

good

hot

cold

meaty

soft

sweet

crunchy

firm

ADJECTIVES

Sugar in the salt shaker!
SALT
Move back one.

AURANTS

MENU

You ate all your vegetables.
Move ahead two.

CHECK
TOTAL

Talking with your mouth full!
Move back one.

A hamburger tastes good.

Corn is healthy.

Spaghetti has sauce.

Look at the chocolate cake.

Bologna is good.

Broccoli is healthy.

Eat the hot fudge sundae.

Peanut butter is good.

I eat french fries.

Eat vanilla pudding.

I like grilled cheese.

Green beans taste good.

Eat pumpkin pie.

A yummy hot dog is good.

Peas are green.

Drink your milk.	I like apple juice.	Tea is hot.	Soft drinks are bubbly.	Lemonade can be sour.
Pizza is yummy.	I love chicken nuggets.	Fish sticks are tasty.	I eat meat loaf.	Tossed salad is crunchy.
Eat the cole slaw.	I like lettuce and tomato.	Order the salad bar.	I ate the potato salad.	Ice cream is cold.

May Sorting Game

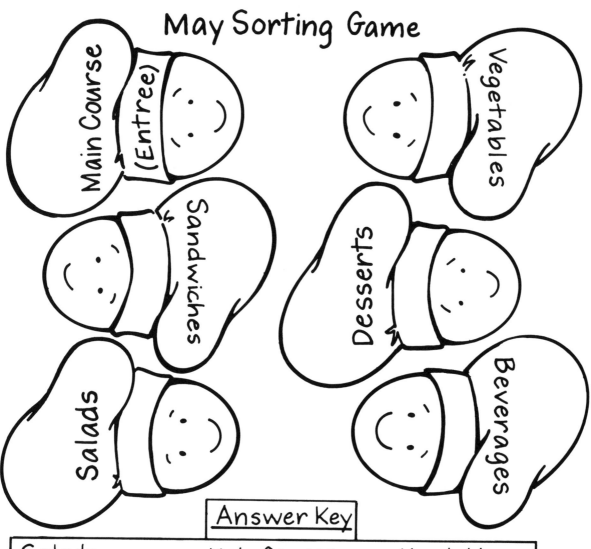

Main Course (Entree)

Vegetables

Sandwiches

Desserts

Salads

Beverages

Answer Key

Salads	Main Course	Vegetables
salad bar	fish sticks	peas
tossed salad	pizza	corn
cole slaw	meat loaf	green beans
potato salad	spaghetti	french fries
lettuce and tomato	chicken nuggets	broccoli

Sandwiches	Desserts	Beverages
hamburger	ice cream	milk
hot dog	pumpkin pie	apple juice
grilled cheese	vanilla pudding	tea
peanut butter	hot fudge sundae	soft drinks
bologna	chocolate cake	lemonade

May Matching Game

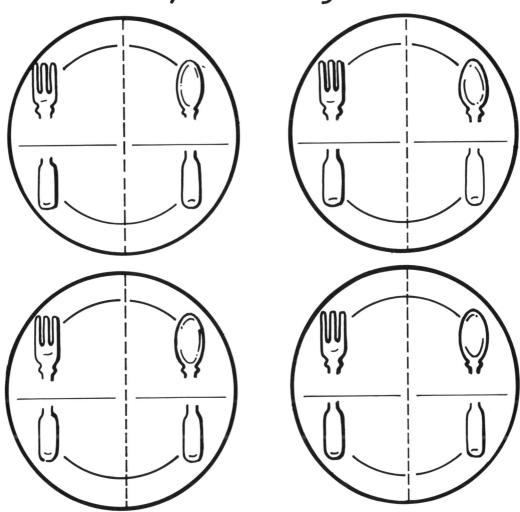

Answer Key

apple + juice	pumpkin + pie
soft + drinks	vanilla + pudding
chicken + nuggets	hot fudge + sundae
fish + sticks	green + beans
meat + loaf	french + fries
salad + bar	hot + dog
cole + slaw	peanut + butter
ice + cream	grilled + cheese

~MENU~

Vegetables

corn
peas
green beans
french fries
broccoli

MainCourse(Entree)

pizza
meat loaf
fish sticks
spaghetti
chicken nuggets

Salads

tossed salad
cole slaw
lettuce and tomato
potato salad
salad bar

Desserts

ice cream
pumpkin pie
vanilla pudding
chocolate cake
hot fudge sundae

Beverages

milk
apple juice
soft drinks
lemonade
tea

Sandwiches

hamburger
hot dog
grilled cheese
peanut butter
bologna

MAY

SUNDAY	MONDAY	TUESDAY	WEDNESDAY	THURSDAY	FRIDAY	SATURDAY

WE LOVE RESTAURANTS

5. LEARNING CENTER SKILL GAMES

In this section you will find reproducible game directions, answer keys, and game cards for assembling 40 hands-on games to use during any theme. There are:

- 8 board games
- 7 card games
- 6 sorting games
- 7 matching games (memory style)
- 12 matching games (puzzle-style)

The section has two parts. Part I shows you how to assemble:

- board games
- card games
- sorting games
- matching games (memory style and puzzle style)

Part II contains:

- reproducible game cards (15 cards per page) for
  —board games
  —card games
  —sorting games
  —memory-style matching games
- reproducible game cards (10 per page) for puzzle-style matching games
- reproducible answer keys
- blank pages for writing your own cards

PART I: ASSEMBLING SKILL GAMES

Board Games

1. Choose any of the following skills to make board games:
   - Abbreviations
   - Antonyms
   - Compound Words

- Contractions
- Figurative Language
- Homophones
- Syllables
- Synonyms

2. Copy and decorate the game board master from any theme.

3. Glue the two board-game halves inside a file folder and trim protruding edges. Write the name of the game on the front of the folder (Antonyms).

4. Copy the game-board directions and glue them on the back of the folder. Write the object of the game in the place provided. Object of the game appears on the answer key page.

5. Copy the skill game-cards (15 cards to a page) on card stock. To add words, copy blank cards (found at the back of this book) and write your own. Laminate the sheets if desired, and cut them apart on the lines to form cards.

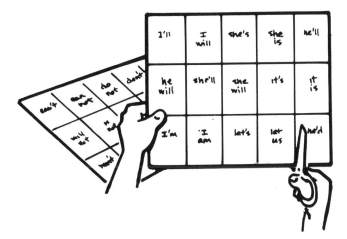

Copy the answer key and glue it on tagboard. Add extra words to the key.

6. Glue a small brown envelope to the back of the folder to hold game cards and the answer key. Laminate the game board for durability. With a sharp knife, slit the envelope open.

GAME-BOARD RULES AND DIRECTIONS

Rules:

Two or three people may play this game. You will need a game board, game cards, an answer key, one die, and a marker for each player.

Object of the game: _____

Directions:

1. Each player picks a marker and places it on *START*.

2. Players roll the die. Player with the highest number will go first. Play clockwise.

3. Each player rolls the die, draws a card, and gives an answer.

4. If the answer is correct the player moves ahead the number shown on the die. If the answer is incorrect the player does not move.

5. Player puts the card at the bottom of the pile.

6. The first player to reach *FINISH* wins!

NOTE: If players do not agree on an answer, they check the answer key.

Card Games

1. The object of the card game is to match pairs of words. Choose any of the following skills to make card games:
   - Abbreviations
   - Antonyms
   - Compound Words
   - Contractions
   - Figurative Language
   - Homophones
   - Synonyms

2. Use both pages of game cards (15 cards to a page) to make a card game. Make one copy of each page on card stock. To add word pairs, copy the blank cards at the back of this book and write your own. Laminate the sheets and cut them apart on the lines to form cards.

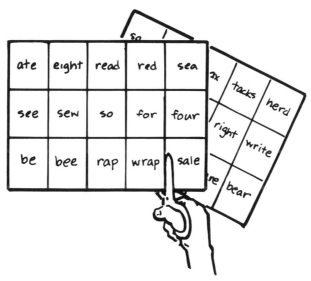

3. Use a small box, a small brown envelope, or a self-sealing plastic bag for storing the cards. Decorate the top of the box or the front of the envelope or bag.

4. Copy the card-game directions and glue them inside the box top or on the back of the envelope.

5. Copy the answer key and glue it on tagboard. Add extra words to the key.

CARD GAME RULES AND DIRECTIONS

Rules:

Two players may play. Players will need game cards and an answer key.

Object of the game: _____

Directions:

1. Deal five cards to each player. Stack the rest of the cards face down.
2. Player 1 draws one card from the rest of the stack. The player then discards 1 unwanted card face up beside the stack.
3. The other player draws 1 card—from the stack or from the top of the discard pile—and then discard 1 unwanted card.
4. When players get a match, they put the pair down on the table.
5. The fist player to lay all his or her cards on the table wins!

NOTE. If players do not agree on an answer, they check the answer key.

Sorting Games

1. Choose any of the following skills to make sorting games:
   - Consonant Blends (4 games)
   - Consonant Digraphs
   - Syllables

2. Copy the skill game-cards (15 cards to a page) on card stock. To add words, copy the blank cards at the back of this book and write your own. Laminate the sheets and cut them apart on the lines to form cards.

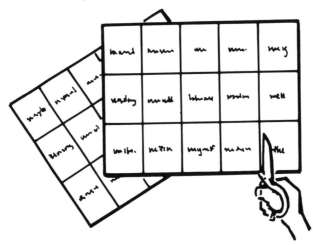

3. Write the names of the sorting categories (1 syllable, 2 syllables, 3 syllables) on index cards. Categories appear on the answer key page. (See object of the game.)

4. Use cylinder containers. Attach the index cards to the top edge of the containers with clothespins or jumbo paper clips.

5. Use a small brown envelope or self-sealing plastic bag for storing the cards.

6. Glue the game directions on the back of the envelope or glue on tagboard and place inside the plastic bag.

7. Copy the answer key and glue it on tagboard. Add extra words to the key. Place the key inside the envelope or plastic bag.

SORTING GAME RULES AND DIRECTIONS

Rules:

One to two players may play this game. You will need game cards, containers, clothespins, index cards and an answer key.

Object of the game: _____

Directions:

1. Look at the game cards. Decide which category each card matches. Put the card in that container.
2. When you have sorted all the cards, get out the answer key.
3. Read the cards to a partner.

Matching Games

1. Choose any of the following skills to make matching games:
   - Abbreviations
   - Antonyms
   - Compound Words
   - Consonant Blends
   - Consonant Digraphs
   - Contractions
   - Figurative Language
   - Homophones
   - Syllables
   - Synonyms

2. For the memory-style game copy skill game-cards (15 cards to a page) on card stock. For the puzzle-style game, copy skill-game cards (10 cards to a page) on card stock. To add words, copy the blank cards at the back of this book and write your own. Laminate the sheets if desired, and cut them apart on the lines to form cards.

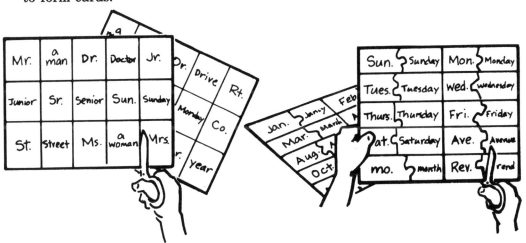

NOTE. Thirty cards are too many for one memory-style game. Make several games by using 3–5 card pairs per game.

3. Decorate a small box, a small brown envelope, or a self-sealing plastic bag for storing the cards.

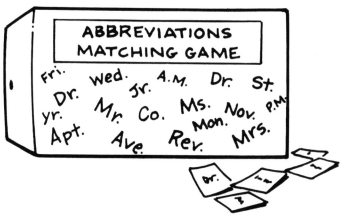

4. Copy the game directions and glue them inside the box top or on the back of the envelope or bag.

5. Copy the answer key and glue it on tagboard. Add extra words to the key. Place the key inside the envelope or plastic bag.

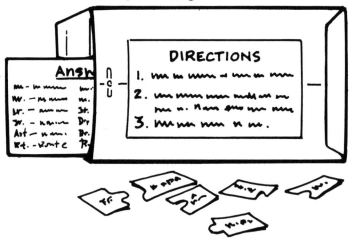

MATCHING GAME RULES AND DIRECTIONS

Rules (Memory Style):

Two or three players may play. Players will need game cards and an answer key.

Object of the game: _____

Directions:

1. Place cards face down in a pattern (three rows of four).
2. Player 1 turns over 2 cards. If the cards show a matching pair, the player may keep the pair. If the cards do not match, the player turns the cards over again.
3. Play continues until all pairs are matched.
4. Players count their cards. The player with the most cards wins!

Rules (Matching Style):

One or two players may play. Players will need puzzle matching cards and an answer key.

Directions:

1. Turn the cards face up so that the words show.
2. Try to find pairs of words that match.

PART II: GAME CARDS AND ANSWER KEYS

Abbreviations

- Board game
  Object: If you draw an abbreviation, name the word. If you draw a word, spell its abbreviation.
- Card game
  Object: Lay down pairs of words and their abbreviations (Dr. + Doctor).
- Matching game (memory or puzzle style)
  Object: Match words with their abbreviations (Sunday + Sun.).

Answer Key

Mr.	a man	Wed.	Wednesday
Ms.	a woman	Thur.	Thursday
Mrs.	a married woman	Fri.	Friday
Dr.	Doctor	Sat.	Saturday
Jr.	Junior	Ave.	Avenue
Sr.	Senior	Blvd.	Boulevard
Rev.	Reverend	Dr.	Drive
Sun.	Sunday	St.	Street
Mon.	Monday	Rt.	Route
Tue.	Tuesday	Apt.	Apartment

Mr.	a man	Ms.

Mrs.	a woman	Junior
Ms.	Doctor	Jr.
a man	Dr.	Reverend
Mr.	a married woman	Rev.
	Sr.	Senior	Sun.

Sunday	Mon.	Monday	Tue.	Tuesday
Wed.	Wednesday	Thur.	Thursday	Fri.
Friday	Sat.	Saturday	Ave.	Avenue

Blvd.	Boulevard	Dr.	Drive	St.
Street	Rt.	Route	Apt.	Apartment

Mr.	**a man**	**Ms.**	**a woman**
Mrs.	**a married woman**	**Dr.**	**Doctor**
Jr.	**Junior**	**Sr.**	**Senior**
Rev.	**Reverend**	**Sun.**	**Sunday**
Mon.	**Monday**	**Tue.**	**Tuesday**

Wed. Wednesday	**Thur.** Thursday
Fri. Friday	**Sat.** Saturday
Ave. Avenue	**Blvd.** Boulevard
Dr. Drive	**St.** Street
Rt. Route	**Apt.** Apartment

Antonyms

- Board game
  Object: Name an antonym for the word you draw.
- Card game
  Object: Lay down pairs of antonyms (hot + cold).
- Matching game (memory or puzzle style)
  Object: Match pairs of antonyms.

Answer Key

young-old	well-sick
noisy-quiet	smile-frown
good-bad	light-dark
useful-useless	mother-father
on-off	first-last
full-empty	dull-sharp
thin-fat or thick	float-sink
warm-cool	play-work
weak-strong	new-old
buy-sell	bad-good

good	quiet	noisy	old	young
off	on	useless	useful	bad
warm	fat or thick	thin	empty	full

sell	light	last
buy	frown	first
strong	smile	father
weak	sick	mother
cool	well	dark

play	good	
sink	bad	
float	old	
sharp	new	
dull	work	

| young | old | noisy | quiet |

| good | bad | useful | useless |

| on | off | full | empty |

| thin | fat or thick | warm | cool |

| weak | strong | buy | sell |

well · sick	smile · frown
light · dark	mother · father
first · last	dull · sharp
float · sink	play · work
new · old	bad · good

Compound Words

- Board game

   Object: Name a compound word made from the word you draw.
- Card game

   Object: Lay down pairs of words that make compound words (some + thing).
- Matching game (memory or puzzle style)

   Object: Match pairs of words that make compound words.

Answer Key

airplane	milkman
baseball	notebook
bookcase	outside
catfish	playground
cowboy	raincoat
forgive	something
grandfather	sunshine
grandmother	today
housework	walkway
into	yourself

book	ball	base
boy	cow	fish
grand	father	grand

plane	air
cat	case
give	for

to	in	work	house	mother
out	book	note	man	milk
coat	rain	ground	play	side

some	thing	sun	shine	to
day	walk	way	your	self

air) plane

base (ball

book ¦ case

cat) fish

cow (boy

for ¦ give

grand) father

grand) mother

house ¦ work

in ¦ to

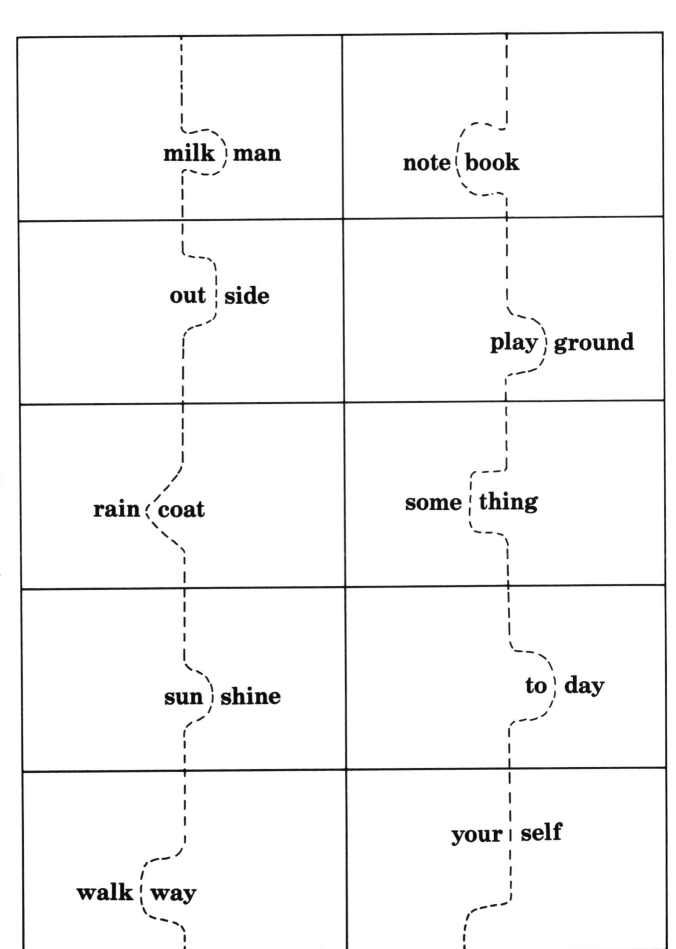

milk) man

note (book

out ⌐ side

play) ground

rain (coat

some ⌐ thing

sun) shine

to) day

walk ⌐ way

your ⌐ self

Consonant Blends

- Sorting game
  Object: Sort words by blend (bl = black, blue, blouse—cl = clock, climb, class, etc.).
- Matching game (puzzle-style)
  Object: Match word parts to make a word (bl + ack).

Answer keys

1 blends: bl, cl, fl, gl, pl, sl

bl	black, blue, blouse, blow, blend
cl	clock, climb, clean, clap, close
fl	floor, flag, fly, flat, flash
gl	glance, glad, glow, glide, glee
pl	play, plate, plow, please, place
sl	sly, slide, sled, slow, slap

r blends: br, cr, dr, fr, gr, pr, tr

br	break, brown, bread, broken, breeze
cr	cream, cracker, crown, cry
dr	dress, dry, drink, drop
fr	frog, friend, from, front
gr	gray, green, grow, gravy
pr	proud, prize, pretty, present
tr	track, train, truck, try, trip

s blends: sc, sk, sm, sn, sp, st, sw

sc	scare, scale, score, school
sk	slate, skip, skunk, skin
sm	smell, smile, small, smoke
sn	snake, snail, snow, sneeze
sp	spell, speak, spot, speed, spade
st	stop, step, steal, still, store
sw	swing, sweat, sweet, swim

Three-letter blends: scr, spr, thr, str, spl, shr

scr   scrap, scrape, screen, scratch

spr   spring, sprout, spray, spread

thr   throw, through, three, thread

str   straw, strike, strong, stress, string

spl   splash, split, splatter, splurge

shr   shrub, shred, shrimp, shrew, shrink

qu   quick, quiet, queen, quite

black	blue	blouse	blow	blend
clock	climb	clean	clap	close
floor	flag	fly	flat	flash

glee	glide	glow
place	please	plow
slap	slow	sled

glad	glance
plate	play
slide	sly

bl) ack

bl (ue

bl (ouse

bl) ow

bl (end

cl (ock

cl) imb

cl) ean

cl (ap

cl (ose

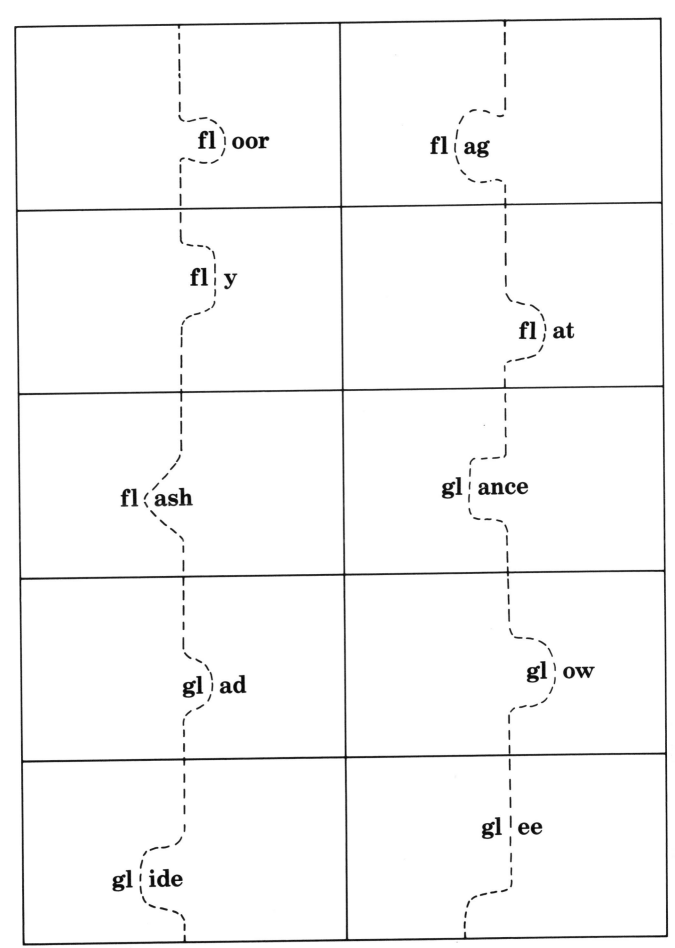

fl oor

fl ag

fl y

fl at

fl ash

gl ance

gl ad

gl ow

gl ide

gl ee

pl ay

pl ate

pl ow

pl ease

pl ace

sl y

sl ide

sl ed

sl ow

sl ap

break	brown	bread	broken	breeze
cream	cracker	crown	cry	dress
dry	drink	drop	frog	friend

grow	green	gray	front	from
present	pretty	prize	proud	gravy
trip	try	truck	train	track

br | eak

br | own

br | ead

br | oken

br | eeze

cr | eam

cr | acker

cr | own

cr | y

dr | ess

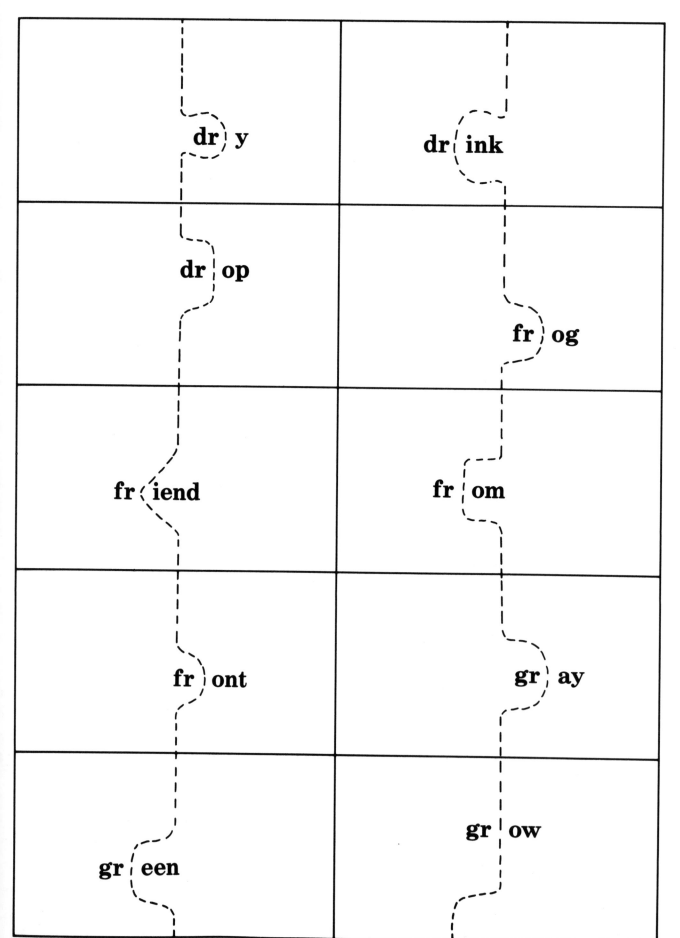

gr avy

pr oud

pr ize

pr etty

pr esent

tr ack

tr ain

tr uck

tr y

tr ip

skate	smile	snow
school	smell	snail
score	skin	snake
scale	skunk	smoke
scare	skip	small

speed	spot	speak
still	steal	step
swim	sweet	sweat

spell	sneeze	
stop	spade	
swing	store	

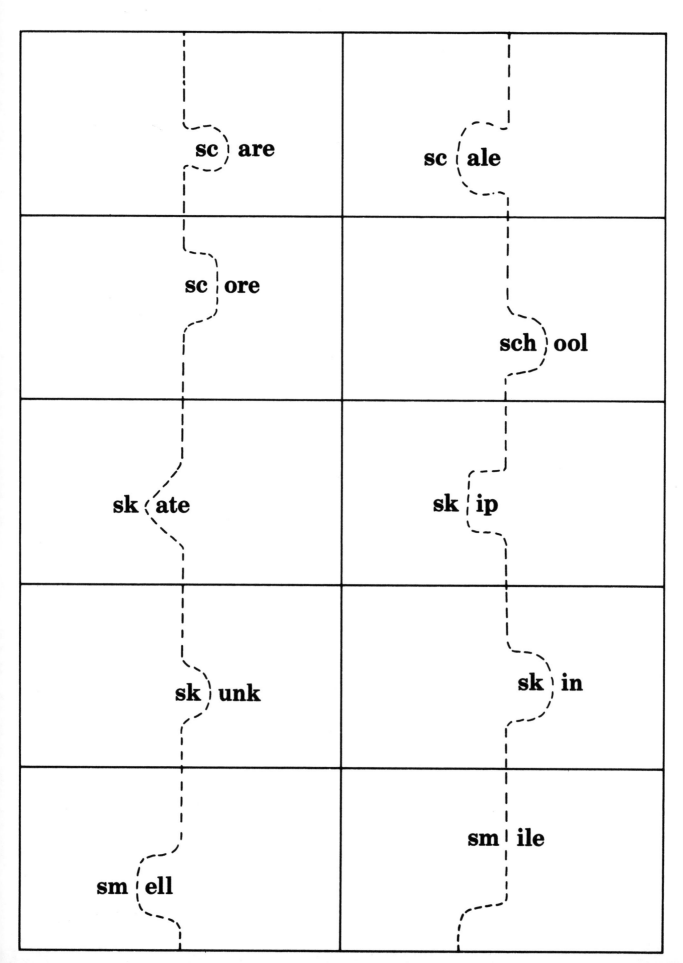

sc) are

sc (ale

sc (ore

sch) ool

sk (ate

sk (ip

sk) unk

sk) in

sm (ell

sm | ile

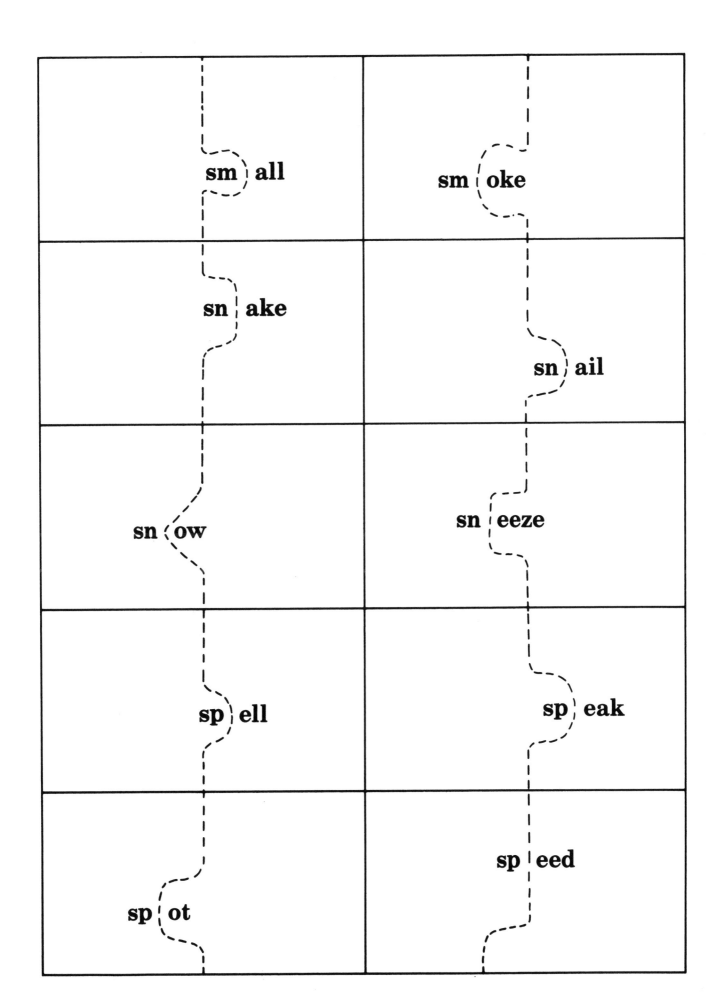

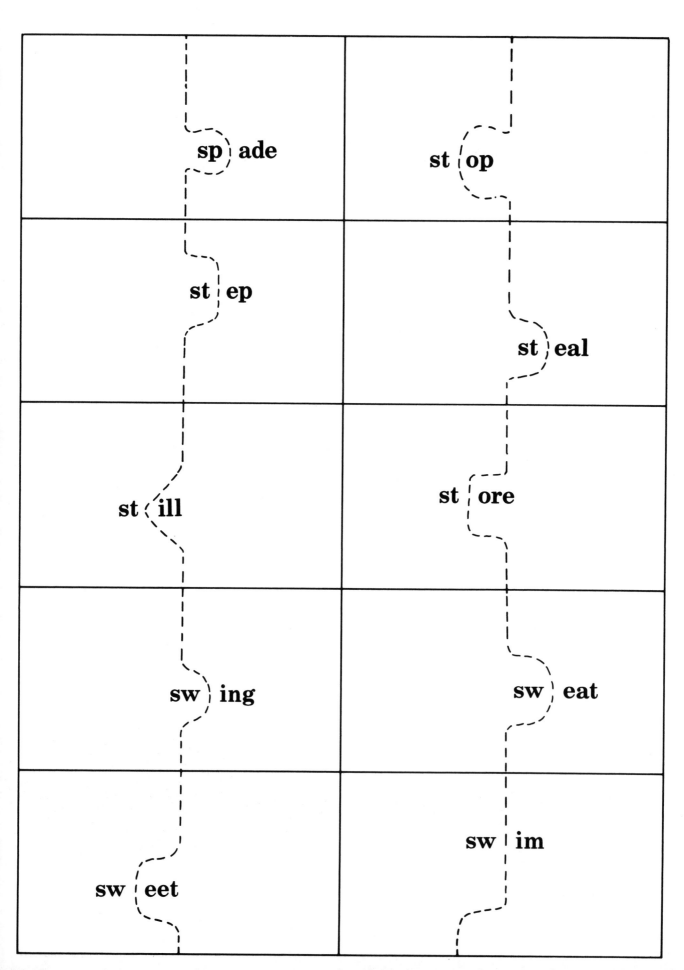

spring	scratch	screen	scrape	scrap
through	throw	spread	spray	sprout
strong	strike	straw	thread	three

splatter	split	splash	string	stress
shrew	shrimp	shred	shrub	splurge
quite	queen	quiet	quick	shrink

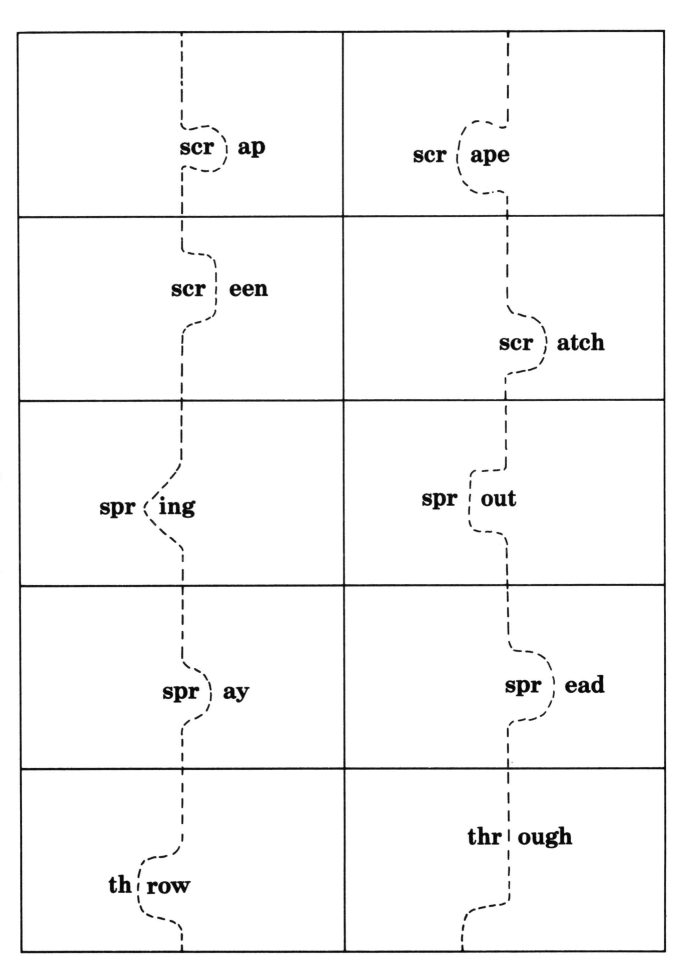

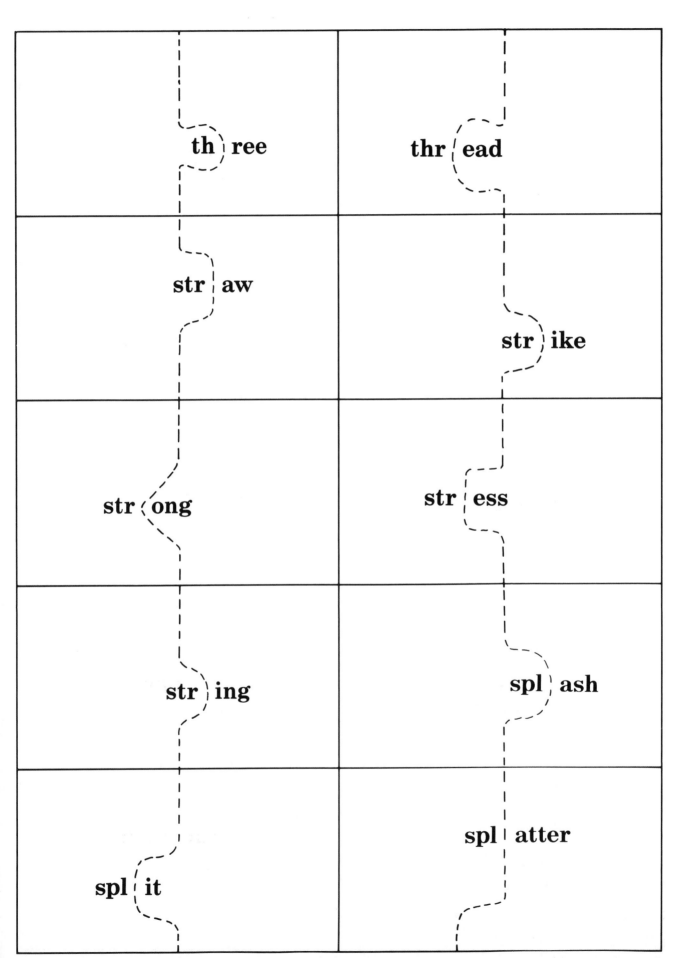

th ree

thr ead

str aw

str ike

str ong

str ess

str ing

spl ash

spl it

spl atter

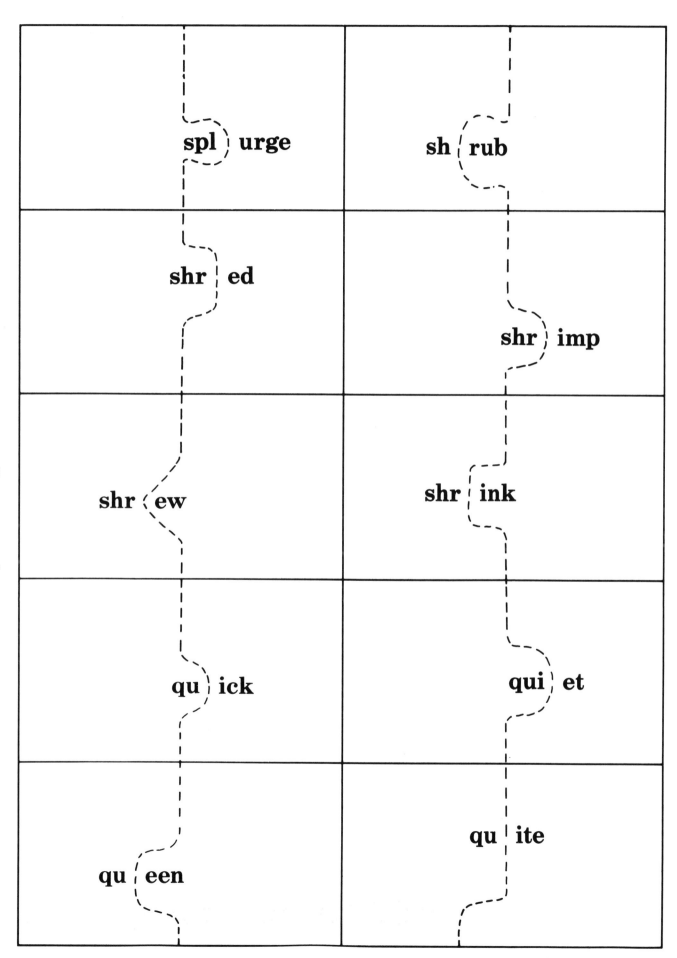

Consonant Digraphs

- Sorting game
  Object: Sort words by digraph (ch = check, chair, itch—sh = shell, shirt, dish, etc.).
- Matching game (puzzle style)
  Object: Match word parts to make a word (sh + ell).

Answer Key

ch	*sh*	*th*	*wh*
children	shirt	thumb	whistle
chicken	shell	Thursday	when
chair	shoe	thirty	wheel
chimney	short	thank	whale
catch	fish	with	where
rich	dish	math	why
hatch	splash	month	
	wish	mouth	
		both	

catch	chimney	chair	chicken	children
shoe	shell	shirt	hatch	rich
wish	splash	dish	fish	short

thumb	Thursday	thirty	thank	with
math	month	mouth	both	whistle
when	wheel	whale	where	why

ch ildren

ch icken

ch air

ch imney

cat **ch**

ri **ch**

hat **ch**

sh irt

sh ell

sh oe

sh) ort

fi (sh

di | sh

spla) sh

wi (sh

th | umb

Th) ursday

th) irty

th (ank

wi | th

ma) th

mon (th

mou | th

bo) th

wh (istle

wh | en

wh) eel

wh) ale

wh | ere

wh | y

Contractions

- Board game

  Object: If you draw a contraction, name two words that make it. If you draw two words, name the contraction.
- Card game

  Object: Lay down pairs of words and contractions (can not + can't).
- Matching game (memory or puzzle style)

  Object: Match words with their contractions (is not + isn't).

Answer Key

can not—can't	I will—I'll
do not—don't	it is—it's
are not—aren't	that is—that's
will not—won't	he is—he's
have not—haven't	let us—let's
is not—isn't	was not—wasn't
has not—hasn't	he will—he'll
would not—wouldn't	here is—here's
did not—didn't	there is—there's
had not—hadn't	you are—you're

are not	haven't	would not
don't	have not	hasn't
do not	won't	has not
can't	will not	isn't
can not	aren't	is not

hadn't	that is	let's
had not	it's	let us
didn't	it is	he's
did not	I'll	he is
wouldn't	I will	that's

here is	he'll	he will
you're	you are	there's

wasn't	was not	
there is	here's	

can not	can't	do not	don't
are not	aren't	will not	won't
have not	haven't	is not	isn't
has not	hasn't	would not	wouldn't
did not	didn't	had not	hadn't

I will	I'll	it is	it's

that is	that's	he is	he's

let us	let's	was not	wasn't

he will	he'll	here is	here's

there is	there's	you are	you're

Figurative Language

- Board game

  Object: Draw a figure of speech, and name its meaning.
- Card game

  Object: Lay down pairs—figures of speech and their meanings (tickled pink + happy).
- Matching game (memory or puzzle style)

  Object: Match figures of speech with their meanings.

Answer Key

skin of my teeth—barely

shake a leg—hurry up

put your best foot forward—use good manners

in a pickle—in trouble

piece of cake—easy

apple of my eye—my favorite person

feeling blue—depressed

tickled pink—happy

green with envy—jealous

raining cats and dogs—a downpour

frog in my throat—hoarse

spring chicken—young person

eats like a bird—light or picky eater

fish out of water—feeling out of place

smell a rat—suspect something

my lips are sealed—I won't tell

off the top of my head—without thinking about it

head in the clouds—day dreaming

foot in my mouth—said the wrong thing

stiff upper lip—be brave

put your best foot forward	easy	tickled pink
hurry up	piece of cake	depressed
shake a leg	in trouble	feeling blue
barely	in a pickle	my favorite person
skin of my teeth	use good manners	apple of my eye

a downpour	eats like a bird	suspect something
raining cats and dogs	young person	smell a rat
jealous	spring chicken	feeling out of place
green with envy	hoarse	fish out of water
happy	frog in my throat	light or picky eater

head in the clouds	be brave	
without thinking about it	stiff upper lip	
off the top of my head	said the wrong thing	
I won't tell	foot in my mouth	
my lips are sealed	day dreaming	

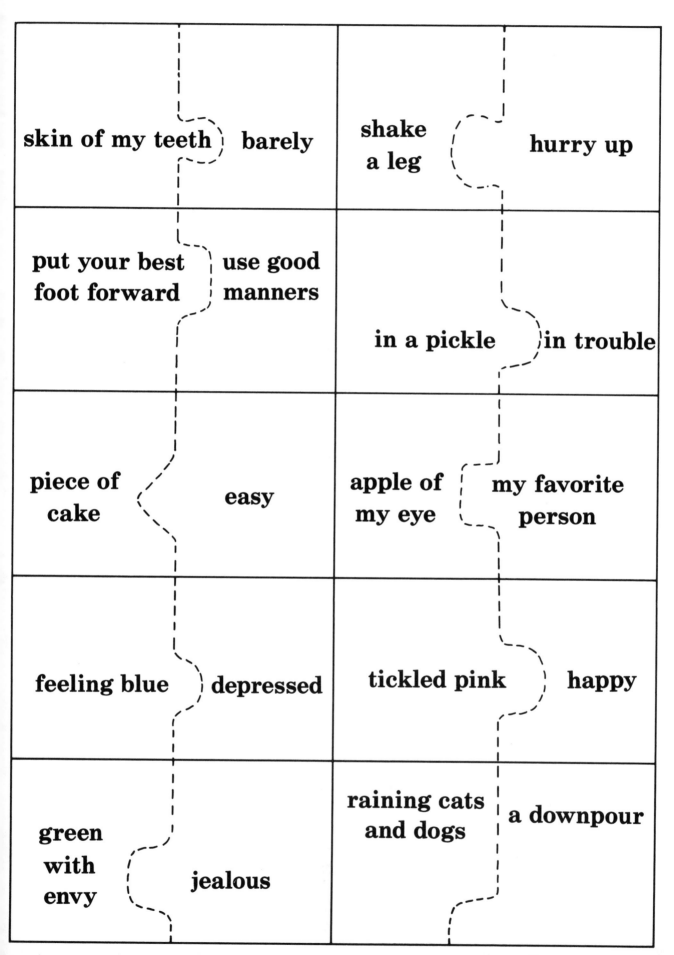

skin of my teeth) barely

shake a leg) hurry up

put your best foot forward) use good manners

in a pickle) in trouble

piece of cake) easy

apple of my eye) my favorite person

feeling blue) depressed

tickled pink) happy

green with envy) jealous

raining cats and dogs) a downpour

frog in my throat	hoarse	spring chicken	young person
eats like a bird	light or picky eater	fish out of water	feeling out of place
smell a rat	suspect something	my lips are sealed	I won't tell
off the top of my head	without thinking about it	head in the clouds	day dreaming
foot in my mouth	said the wrong thing	stiff upper lip	be brave

Homophones

- Board game
  Object: Name meaning of the homophone you draw.
- Card game
  Object: Lay down pairs of homophones (pear + pair).
- Matching game (memory or puzzle style)
  Object: Match pairs of homophones.

Answer Key

hair-hare	hi-high
tail-tale	told-tolled
hay-hey	hoarse-horse
tea-tee	hole-whole
heal-heel	cell-sell
to-two-too	ring-wring
hear-here	cent-sent
tow-toe	root-route
heard-herd	chili-chilly
their-there-they're	sail-sale

hay	tale	tail
heel	heal	tee
here	hear	too

hare	hair
tea	hey
two	to

their	herd	heard	toe	tow
told	high	hi	they're	there
whole	hole	horse	hoarse	tolled

cent	wring	ring	sell	cell
chilly	chili	route	root	sent
			sale	sail

hair	hare	tail	tale
hay	hey	tea	tee
heal	heel	to	two
hear	here	tow	toe
heard	herd	their	there

hi high	told tolled
hoarse horse	hole whole
cell sell	ring wring
cent sent	root route
chili chilly	sail sale

Syllables

- Board game
  Object: Name the number of syllables for the word you draw.
- Sorting game
  Object: Sort words by number of syllables in the word (1 Syllable = is, far, less—2 Syllables = almost, someone, without, etc.).

Answer Key

One Syllable	Two Syllables	Three Syllables
boy	almost	fishermen
her	someone	imagine
pet	sunshine	beautiful
shape	without	together
moon	picture	elephant
door	around	Saturday
smell	shoelace	bicycle
mouth	farmer	hummingbird
fast	princess	understand
send	follow	
black		

moon	shape	pet
send	fast	mouth
without	sunshine	someone

her	boy
smell	door
almost	black

princess	farmer	shoelace
together	beautiful	imagine
understand	hummingbird	bicycle
around	picture	
fisherman	follow	
Saturday	elephant	

Synonyms

- Board game
  Object: Name a synonym for the word you draw.
- Card game
  Object: Lay down pairs of synonyms (pretty + beautiful).
- Matching game (memory or puzzle style)
  Object: Match pairs of synonyms.

Answer Key

big-large	quiet-still
near-close	happy-jolly
fast-quick	neat-tidy
fix-repair	harm-hurt
ship-boat	join-connect
crawl-creep	allow-permit
gift-present	unfasten-loosen
easy-simple	nearest-closest
pretty-cute	brave-fearless
forest-woods	blend-mix

fast	close	near	large	big
boat	ship	repair	fix	quick
easy	present	gift	creep	crawl

woods	forest	cute
neat	jolly	happy
connect	join	hurt

pretty	simple
still	quiet
harm	tidy

allow	permit	unfasten	loosen	nearest
closest	brave	fearless	blend	mix

big — large	near — close
fast — quick	fix — repair
ship — boat	crawl — creep
gift — present	easy — simple
pretty — cute	forest — woods

quiet	still	happy	jolly
neat	tidy	harm	hurt
join	connect	allow	permit
unfasten	loosen	nearest	closest
brave	fearless	blend	mix

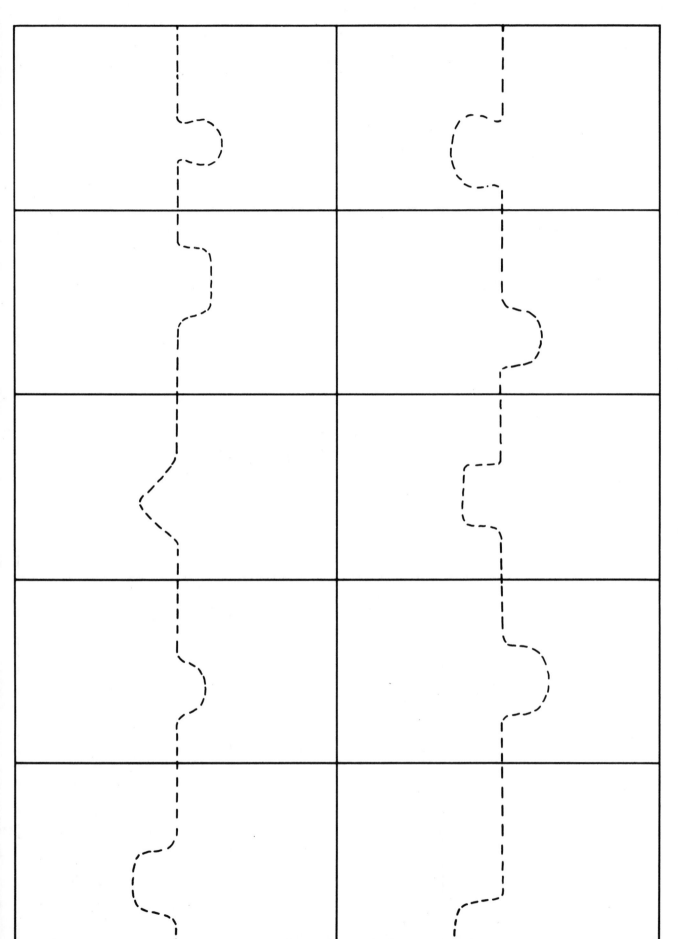